I0017294

# Table of Contents

Chapter 1: The Essence of Programming Languages.................................................16

1.1 Understanding Programming Language Fundamentals.......................................16

1.2 Evolution of Programming Languages ................................................................17

1.3 Common Features of C, C++, Java, JavaScript, and Python...............................19

1.4 High-Level vs. Low-Level Languages..................................................................20

1.5 The Role of a Compiler and Interpreter ............................................................22

Chapter 2: Decoding C: The Ancestor of Modern Languages ................................25

2.1 The Birth and Philosophy of C...........................................................................25

2.2 Structure of a C Program ..................................................................................26

2.3 Memory Management in C .................................................................................28

2.4 C's Contribution to Operating Systems and Software.......................................30

2.5 Limitations and Legacy of C...............................................................................32

Chapter 3: C++: Bridging Procedural and Object-Oriented Programming...........34

3.1 The Evolution from C to C++..............................................................................34

3.2 Core Concepts of Object-Oriented Programming in C++ ..................................36

3.3 Memory Management: From Malloc to Constructors .......................................39

3.4 The Standard Template Library (STL)..................................................................42

3.5 Real-world Applications of C++ .........................................................................44

Chapter 4: Java: Write Once, Run Anywhere........................................................48

4.1 Java's Answer to Cross-Platform Compatibility.................................................48

4.2 Understanding Java Virtual Machine (JVM).......................................................50

4.3 Object-Oriented Principles in Java ....................................................................52

4.4 Garbage Collection in Java.................................................................................55

4.5 Java in Enterprise Solutions ..............................................................................57

Chapter 5: JavaScript: The Language of the Web .................................................60

5.1 From Simple Scripts to Rich Web Applications .................................................60

5.2 Understanding the DOM and Browser Rendering.............................................62

5.3 Event-Driven Programming in JavaScript..........................................................64

5.4 Asynchronous Programming and Callbacks ......................................................66

5.5 The Rise of Node.js and Server-Side JavaScript ...............................................68

Chapter 6: Python: The Language of Simplicity and Elegance.............................71

6.1 Python's Philosophy and Design Principles .......................................................71

6.2 Python's Interpreter and Dynamic Typing ...........................................................................72

Interactive Mode ...........................................................................................................................72

Script Execution ...........................................................................................................................72

Dynamic Typing ...........................................................................................................................73

Strong Typing ...............................................................................................................................73

Summary .......................................................................................................................................73

6.3 Libraries and Frameworks in Python .................................................................................73

Standard Library ...........................................................................................................................74

NumPy ..........................................................................................................................................74

Pandas ..........................................................................................................................................74

Matplotlib......................................................................................................................................75

Flask ..............................................................................................................................................75

Django...........................................................................................................................................75

6.4 Python in Data Science and AI...........................................................................................76

Data Science with Python............................................................................................................76

AI and Machine Learning ............................................................................................................76

Jupyter Notebooks .......................................................................................................................77

Conclusion ....................................................................................................................................77

6.5 Scripting, Automation, and Web Development with Python ..........................................77

Scripting.........................................................................................................................................78

Automation....................................................................................................................................78

Web Development.........................................................................................................................79

Conclusion ....................................................................................................................................79

7.1 Understanding Syntax in Programming Languages ........................................................81

Importance of Syntax....................................................................................................................81

Syntax Elements............................................................................................................................81

1. Keywords ..................................................................................................................................81

2. Operators...................................................................................................................................81

3. Variables ...................................................................................................................................82

4. Statements.................................................................................................................................82

5. Brackets and Delimiters...........................................................................................................82

Language-Specific Syntax.............................................................................................................82

Syntax Errors.................................................................................................................................82

Conclusion ....................................................................................................................................82

7.2 The Role of Semantics in Code Execution.................................................83

Understanding Semantics...................................................................................83

Key Aspects of Semantics..................................................................................83

Language-Specific Semantics ..........................................................................83

Handling Semantic Errors.................................................................................84

Importance of Semantics...................................................................................84

7.3 Comparing Syntax Across Different Languages........................................84

Syntax Diversity ...................................................................................................84

Benefits of Syntax Diversity .............................................................................85

Challenges of Syntax Diversity........................................................................85

Cross-Language Development .........................................................................85

7.4 Error Handling and Debugging...................................................................86

Error Handling.......................................................................................................86

Debugging...............................................................................................................87

Challenges and Best Practices........................................................................87

7.5 Best Practices for Readable and Maintainable Code .........................88

1. Meaningful Variable and Function Names...............................................88

2. Consistent Indentation and Formatting..................................................88

3. Comments and Documentation ...............................................................88

4. Modularization.................................................................................................89

5. Avoid Magic Numbers and Hardcoding ................................................89

6. Version Control and Collaboration ..........................................................90

7. Unit Testing......................................................................................................90

8. Refactoring ......................................................................................................90

9. Follow Language Best Practices ...............................................................90

Chapter 8: Data Types and Structures .............................................................91

8.1 Primitive Data Types Across Languages..................................................91

Integer Types.........................................................................................................91

Floating-Point Types...........................................................................................91

Boolean Type.........................................................................................................92

Character Types ...................................................................................................92

Conclusion ..............................................................................................................93

8.2 Complex Data Structures and Their Implementation ........................93

Arrays .......................................................................................................................93

Lists (Dynamic Arrays) ................................................................................................94

Linked Lists ...................................................................................................................94

Conclusion ....................................................................................................................95

8.3 Memory Allocation for Data Types.................................................................................96

Stack and Heap Allocation ..........................................................................................96

Automatic vs. Manual Memory Management...........................................................96

Garbage Collection Mechanisms ...............................................................................97

Conclusion ....................................................................................................................97

8.4 Comparing Data Handling in C, C++, Java, JavaScript, and Python .......................97

C........................................................................................................................................97

C++ ..................................................................................................................................98

Java..................................................................................................................................98

JavaScript .......................................................................................................................98

Python .............................................................................................................................99

8.5 Efficient Data Manipulation Techniques......................................................................99

C and C++ .......................................................................................................................99

Java..................................................................................................................................100

JavaScript.......................................................................................................................100

Python.............................................................................................................................100

General Tips ...................................................................................................................101

Chapter 9: Control Structures and Flow .................................................................................102

9.1 Understanding Conditional Statements .......................................................................102

The If Statement..........................................................................................................102

The Switch Statement.................................................................................................103

The Ternary Operator.................................................................................................103

Conditional Statements Best Practices...................................................................103

9.2 Loop Constructs Across Different Languages ..............................................................104

The For Loop.................................................................................................................104

The While Loop.............................................................................................................105

The Do-While Loop ......................................................................................................106

9.3 Recursive Functions and Their Usage...........................................................................106

Recursive Functions in C and C++ ............................................................................106

Recursive Functions in Java ......................................................................................107

Recursive Functions in JavaScript............................................................................108

Recursive Functions in Python ...................................................................109

9.4 Exception Handling and Flow Control .................................................109

Exception Handling in C++ .......................................................................109

Exception Handling in Java.......................................................................110

Exception Handling in JavaScript.............................................................110

Exception Handling in Python...................................................................111

9.5 Writing Efficient and Effective Control Structures.............................111

Optimizing Conditional Statements..........................................................111

Loop Optimization......................................................................................112

Avoiding Nested Loops...............................................................................112

Using Break and Continue Judiciously.....................................................112

Regular Code Reviews and Profiling .........................................................113

Choosing the Right Data Structures..........................................................113

Chapter 10: Object-Oriented Programming Across Languages...............114

10.1 Core Concepts of OOP: Encapsulation, Inheritance, Polymorphism ...........114

1. Encapsulation ........................................................................................114

2. Inheritance.............................................................................................114

3. Polymorphism ........................................................................................115

10.2 Comparing OOP in C++, Java, and Python .....................................115

C++ .............................................................................................................116

Java.............................................................................................................116

Python.........................................................................................................117

10.3 Design Patterns and Best Practices ................................................118

C++ .............................................................................................................118

Java.............................................................................................................119

Python.........................................................................................................119

10.4 The Impact of OOP on Software Development .................................120

Encapsulation and Modularity...................................................................120

Inheritance and Code Reuse......................................................................120

Polymorphism and Flexibility....................................................................121

Encapsulation of State and Behavior.........................................................121

Software Design Patterns...........................................................................121

Challenges and Criticisms .........................................................................121

10.5 Challenges and Criticisms of OOP...................................................122

Complex Class Hierarchies..................................................................................122

Tight Coupling...............................................................................................122

Overhead and Performance..............................................................................123

Difficulty in Learning......................................................................................123

Not Always the Best Fit...................................................................................123

Chapter 11: Functional Programming: A Paradigm Shift.............................................125

Section 11.1: Introduction to Functional Programming.........................................125

Advantages of Functional Programming...........................................................125

Functional Features in Python and JavaScript....................................................125

Section 11.2: Functional Features in Python and JavaScript...................................126

Python and Functional Programming................................................................126

JavaScript and Functional Programming...........................................................127

Section 11.3: Comparing Imperative and Functional Approaches............................128

Imperative Programming................................................................................128

Functional Programming................................................................................128

When to Choose Each Approach......................................................................129

Section 11.4: Use Cases for Functional Programming..........................................129

1. Data Transformation and Processing.............................................................129

2. Parallel and Concurrent Programming..........................................................130

3. Complex Mathematical Calculations.............................................................130

4. Handling Streams and Events......................................................................130

5. Domain-Specific Languages (DSLs)..............................................................131

Section 11.5: The Future of Functional Programming..........................................131

1. Wider Adoption in Mainstream Languages.....................................................131

2. Functional-First Languages.........................................................................131

3. Reactive and Event-Driven Systems.............................................................132

4. Advances in Type Systems.........................................................................132

5. Functional for Data Science and AI..............................................................132

6. Functional in Blockchain and Smart Contracts...............................................132

Chapter 12: Memory Management Across Languages..............................................134

Section 12.1: Understanding Stack and Heap Allocation.......................................134

Stack Allocation...........................................................................................134

Heap Allocation...........................................................................................134

Choosing Between Stack and Heap..................................................................134

Section 12.2: Automatic vs Manual Memory Management .......................................................135

Automatic Memory Management (Garbage Collection) .......................................................135

Manual Memory Management ...................................................................................................136

Choosing Between Approaches ................................................................................................136

Section 12.3: Garbage Collection Mechanisms in Java and Python.................................136

Garbage Collection in Java.......................................................................................................136

Garbage Collection in Python ..................................................................................................137

Section 12.4: Memory Leaks and Management in C and C++..............................................138

Memory Leaks in C and C++.....................................................................................................138

Management Strategies in C and C++......................................................................................139

Section 12.5: Best Practices for Efficient Memory Usage...................................................139

1. Use Stack Memory When Appropriate ...............................................................................140

2. Limit Dynamic Memory Allocation.......................................................................................140

3. Avoid Memory Leaks .............................................................................................................140

4. Use RAII in C++......................................................................................................................140

5. Employ Smart Pointers (C++)...............................................................................................140

6. Profile and Optimize ..............................................................................................................141

7. Avoid Global Variables...........................................................................................................141

8. Check Return Values of Allocation Functions...................................................................141

9. Release Resources in Error Handling Paths .....................................................................141

Chapter 13: Concurrency and Parallelism .................................................................................142

Section 13.1: Basics of Concurrency and Parallelism .......................................................142

Concurrency...............................................................................................................................142

Parallelism ..................................................................................................................................142

Section 13.2: Multithreading in Java and C++ .....................................................................143

Java Multithreading...................................................................................................................143

C++ Multithreading....................................................................................................................144

Section 13.3: Asynchronous Programming in JavaScript and Python ...........................145

Asynchronous Programming in JavaScript...........................................................................145

Asynchronous Programming in Python..................................................................................146

Section 13.4: Synchronization and Race Conditions .........................................................148

Synchronization Mechanisms..................................................................................................148

Race Conditions ........................................................................................................................149

Section 13.5: Real-World Applications of Concurrent Programming................................150

1. Web Servers ..................................................................................................150

2. Video Game Engines ...................................................................................150

3. Database Systems .......................................................................................150

4. Operating Systems......................................................................................150

5. Parallel Computing.....................................................................................150

6. Networking ..................................................................................................151

7. Financial Systems.......................................................................................151

8. IoT (Internet of Things)............................................................................151

9. Video Streaming .........................................................................................151

10. Search Engines..........................................................................................151

Chapter 14: Libraries, Frameworks, and APIs ..........................................151

    Section 14.1: The Role of Libraries in Software Development................151

Section 14.2: Popular Frameworks for Web Development........................153

Section 14.3: API Integration and Management........................................154

    The Significance of API Integration.........................................................154

    API Management ........................................................................................155

    Popular API Management Tools................................................................155

Section 14.4: Cross-Language Compatibility and Bridging .....................156

    Why Cross-Language Compatibility Matters ...........................................156

    Techniques for Cross-Language Compatibility........................................157

    Challenges in Cross-Language Compatibility ..........................................157

Section 14.5: Evaluating and Choosing the Right Tools...........................158

    The Importance of Tool Selection.............................................................158

    Evaluating Tools.........................................................................................158

    Making the Decision ..................................................................................160

Chapter 15: Debugging and Testing ...........................................................161

Section 15.1: Principles of Effective Debugging ......................................161

    1. Reproduce the Issue .............................................................................161

    2. Understand the Code ............................................................................161

    3. Use Version Control .............................................................................161

    4. Start with Assertions ............................................................................161

    5. Divide and Conquer.............................................................................161

    6. Use Debugging Tools ...........................................................................161

    7. Replicate the Environment...................................................................162

8. Keep a Log................................................................................................162

9. Collaborate and Seek Help................................................................162

10. Test Your Fixes..................................................................................162

11. Document the Solution....................................................................162

Section 15.2: Unit Testing and Test-Driven Development........................162

What is Unit Testing?..............................................................................163

Benefits of Unit Testing.........................................................................163

Test-Driven Development (TDD)..........................................................163

Example of TDD......................................................................................163

Section 15.3: Debugging Tools and Techniques for Each Language........164

Python.......................................................................................................164

Java.............................................................................................................165

C and C++..................................................................................................165

JavaScript..................................................................................................165

Best Practices for Debugging................................................................166

Section 15.4: Integration and System Testing...........................................166

Integration Testing.................................................................................166

System Testing........................................................................................167

Best Practices for Integration and System Testing...........................168

Section 15.5: Building a Robust Testing Framework................................168

Key Considerations for a Testing Framework....................................169

Best Practices for Building a Testing Framework..............................169

Example Testing Framework (Python with PyTest)..........................170

Chapter 16: Version Control and Collaboration........................................172

Section 16.1: Introduction to Version Control Systems..........................172

What Is Version Control?.......................................................................172

Types of Version Control Systems.......................................................172

Advantages of Version Control Systems.............................................172

Section 16.2: Collaborative Coding with Git.............................................173

Understanding Git Basics......................................................................173

Collaborative Workflows.......................................................................174

Setting Up Git for Collaboration........................................................174

Section 16.3: Best Practices for Team Development.................................175

1. Clear and Consistent Code Style.....................................................175

2. Version Control Etiquette...........................................................................175

3. Code Reviews...........................................................................................175

4. Automated Testing....................................................................................175

5. Documentation.........................................................................................176

6. Use of Branching Strategies......................................................................176

7. Continuous Integration and Deployment (CI/CD)......................................176

8. Communication.........................................................................................176

9. Security Best Practices..............................................................................176

10. Code Ownership and Responsibility.........................................................176

11. Continuous Learning...............................................................................176

12. Feedback and Retrospectives..................................................................176

Section 16.4: Code Reviews and Quality Assurance......................................177

Why Code Reviews Matter............................................................................177

Best Practices for Code Reviews...................................................................177

Section 16.5: Managing Large Codebases Across Teams................................178

Challenges of Large Codebases....................................................................179

Strategies for Managing Large Codebases...................................................179

Chapter 17: Optimization and Performance Tuning.......................................181

Section 17.1: Analyzing and Improving Code Performance...........................181

The Importance of Code Performance..........................................................181

Profiling and Analysis..................................................................................181

Optimization Strategies...............................................................................181

Continuous Monitoring and Testing.............................................................182

Section 17.2: Profiling Tools and Techniques...............................................183

Types of Profiling Tools...............................................................................183

Profiling Techniques....................................................................................183

Profiling Best Practices................................................................................184

Section 17.3: Memory Optimization Strategies.............................................184

1. Data Structures Selection.........................................................................184

2. Object Pooling.........................................................................................185

3. Lazy Loading............................................................................................185

4. Memory-Mapped Files..............................................................................185

5. Garbage Collection Optimization.............................................................185

6. Memory Profiling.....................................................................................185

7. Dispose of Resources Properly ...............................................................185

8. Minimize Copying ...................................................................................186

9. Compact Data Structures .......................................................................186

10. Monitoring and Profiling.......................................................................186

Section 17.4: Optimizing CPU Usage and Efficiency ...................................186

1. Algorithm Selection................................................................................186

2. Data Structure Optimization .................................................................187

3. Caching ...................................................................................................187

4. Multithreading and Parallelism .............................................................187

5. Profile and Optimize Hotspots ..............................................................188

6. Batch Processing ....................................................................................188

7. Compiler and Language Features ...........................................................188

8. Minimize I/O Operations........................................................................188

9. Use Lazy Evaluation ...............................................................................188

Section 17.5: Balancing Readability and Performance...............................188

1. Code Comments and Documentation ....................................................189

2. Descriptive Variable and Function Names..............................................189

3. Modularization.......................................................................................189

4. Code Formatting and Style Guides ........................................................190

5. Avoid Premature Optimization ..............................................................190

6. Maintainability over Micro-Optimizations ............................................190

7. Code Reviews..........................................................................................190

8. Testing and Test-Driven Development (TDD)..........................................190

9. Code Refactoring ....................................................................................190

Chapter 18: The Future of Programming Languages...................................192

Section 18.1: Emerging Trends in Software Development...........................192

1. Machine Learning Integration ...............................................................192

2. Quantum Computing Languages ...........................................................192

3. WebAssembly (Wasm) ...........................................................................192

4. Rust for System-Level Programming .....................................................192

5. Domain-Specific Languages (DSLs).........................................................192

6. Low-Code and No-Code Platforms.........................................................193

7. Concurrency and Parallelism..................................................................193

8. Ethical and Sustainable Programming...................................................193

11

9. Continued Evolution of Existing Languages ..................................................193

10. Interoperability ..................................................................................................193

Section 18.2: The Evolution of Programming Paradigms ................................194

1. Procedural Programming ...................................................................................194

2. Object-Oriented Programming (OOP)..............................................................194

3. Functional Programming...................................................................................194

4. Logic Programming.............................................................................................195

5. Event-Driven and Reactive Programming .....................................................195

6. Concurrent and Parallel Programming ..........................................................195

7. Domain-Specific Languages (DSLs)..................................................................196

8. Low-Code and No-Code Paradigms..................................................................196

9. Hybrid Approaches ............................................................................................196

Section 18.3: Predictions for C, C++, Java, JavaScript, and Python ...............197

1. C and C++..............................................................................................................197

2. Java .......................................................................................................................197

3. JavaScript.............................................................................................................197

4. Python ..................................................................................................................198

5. Cross-Language Interoperability .....................................................................198

6. The Impact of AI .................................................................................................198

Section 18.4: The Role of AI in Programming...................................................198

1. Automated Code Generation ............................................................................198

2. Code Review and Quality Assurance ...............................................................199

3. Bug Detection and Predictive Maintenance...................................................199

4. Optimizing Code Performance .........................................................................199

5. Natural Language Interfaces for Coding .........................................................199

6. Challenges and Ethical Considerations...........................................................199

Section 18.5: Preparing for the Next Generation of Languages.....................200

1. Stay Informed .....................................................................................................200

2. Learn Multiple Paradigms.................................................................................200

3. Master Fundamentals........................................................................................200

4. Experiment with New Languages ....................................................................200

5. Open Source Contribution................................................................................201

6. Adopt Modern Development Practices............................................................201

7. Cross-Platform Development ...........................................................................201

8. Consider Domain-Specific Languages (DSLs)................................................201

9. Ethical Considerations................................................201

10. Foster a Growth Mindset................................................201

Section 19.1: Case Studies of Successful Projects in Each Language................................................202

1. Linux Kernel (C)................................................202

2. Facebook (PHP and Hack)................................................202

3. Netflix (Java)................................................202

4. Twitter (Scala)................................................203

5. Instagram (Python)................................................203

6. SpaceX (C++, Python)................................................203

Section 19.2: Cross-Disciplinary Use of Programming Languages................................................203

1. Bioinformatics (Python and R)................................................204

2. Finance (Java and C++)................................................204

3. Geographic Information Systems (GIS) (Python and JavaScript)................................................204

4. Artificial Intelligence (AI) (Python and TensorFlow)................................................205

5. Digital Art (Processing and JavaScript)................................................205

Section 19.3: Large-Scale Systems and Their Challenges................................................205

1. Scalability................................................206

2. Availability and Reliability................................................206

3. Data Management................................................206

4. Security and Privacy................................................206

5. Performance Optimization................................................206

6. Monitoring and Analytics................................................207

7. Cost Management................................................207

8. Maintainability and DevOps................................................207

Section 19.4: Open Source Contributions and Community Impact................................................207

1. The Open Source Movement................................................207

2. Benefits of Open Source Contributions................................................208

3. Popular Open Source Projects................................................208

4. Contributing to Open Source................................................208

5. GitHub and Collaboration Platforms................................................208

6. Licensing and Legal Considerations................................................209

7. Community Etiquette................................................209

8. Impact of Open Source................................................209

Section 19.5: Lessons Learned from Industry Giants ..........................................209

1. Continuous Learning and Adaptation ..........................................209

2. User-Centric Design ..........................................209

3. Iterative Development ..........................................210

4. Automation and DevOps ..........................................210

5. Data-Driven Decision Making ..........................................210

6. Scalability and Performance ..........................................210

7. Security and Privacy ..........................................210

8. Collaboration and Communication ..........................................210

9. Diversity and Inclusion ..........................................210

10. Ethical Considerations ..........................................211

Chapter 20: The Programmer's Journey: Learning and Mastering Languages ..........................................212

Section 20.1: Strategies for Learning New Programming Languages ..........................................212

1. Start with Fundamentals ..........................................212

2. Choose the Right Language ..........................................212

3. Utilize Online Resources ..........................................212

4. Hands-On Practice ..........................................212

5. Work on Real Projects ..........................................212

6. Learn Language Features ..........................................212

7. Read Code and Documentation ..........................................213

8. Join Coding Communities ..........................................213

9. Experiment and Tinker ..........................................213

10. Teach Others ..........................................213

11. Stay Persistent and Patient ..........................................213

12. Stay Updated ..........................................213

Section 20.2: Balancing Breadth and Depth in Language Proficiency ..........................................213

Breadth: Exploring Multiple Languages ..........................................214

Depth: Mastering a Single Language ..........................................214

Section 20.3: Building a Personal Coding Portfolio ..........................................215

Why Build a Coding Portfolio? ..........................................215

How to Build an Effective Portfolio ..........................................216

Section 20.4: Staying Current with Technological Advances ..........................................217

1. Continuous Learning ..........................................217

2. Follow Industry Trends ..........................................217

3. Attend Conferences and Meetups ................................................................217

4. Join Online Communities ...........................................................................218

5. Experiment with Side Projects ...................................................................218

6. Read Books and Documentation ...............................................................218

7. Online Courses and Tutorials.....................................................................218

8. Contribute to Open Source.........................................................................218

9. Follow Thought Leaders .............................................................................218

10. Build a Personal Learning Plan ...............................................................218

11. Embrace New Challenges..........................................................................218

12. Network with Peers....................................................................................218

13. Stay Inquisitive...........................................................................................219

Section 20.5: Fostering a Lifelong Passion for Coding.................................219

1. Build Meaningful Projects .........................................................................219

2. Collaborate with Others ............................................................................219

3. Stay Curious.................................................................................................219

4. Teach and Mentor .......................................................................................219

5. Participate in Coding Challenges..............................................................219

6. Explore Different Domains ........................................................................220

7. Read and Write Code Regularly ................................................................220

8. Attend Tech Events .....................................................................................220

9. Set Personal Goals......................................................................................220

10. Celebrate Your Achievements..................................................................220

11. Stay Informed.............................................................................................220

12. Balance Work and Life ..............................................................................220

13. Join Coding Communities........................................................................220

14. Explore Creative Coding...........................................................................220

15. Keep a Coding Journal ..............................................................................221

# Chapter 1: The Essence of Programming Languages

## 1.1 Understanding Programming Language Fundamentals

Programming languages are the foundation of software development, enabling us to communicate our intentions to computers effectively. They serve as a bridge between human-readable code and machine-executable instructions. In this section, we'll explore the fundamental concepts that underpin all programming languages.

At its core, a programming language is a formalized set of rules and syntax that allows developers to give instructions to a computer. These instructions can range from simple arithmetic calculations to complex data manipulations and control flow.

**Syntax and Semantics:** The two key aspects of any programming language are syntax and semantics. Syntax defines the structure and grammar of the language, specifying how code should be written to be considered valid. Semantics, on the other hand, dictate the meaning of the code and how it should be executed. Understanding and mastering both syntax and semantics are crucial for effective programming.

**Variables and Data Types:** In programming, variables are used to store and manipulate data. Data types define the kind of data a variable can hold, such as integers, floating-point numbers, strings, or custom-defined types. For example, in Python:

```python
# Variable declaration
age = 25

# Data type: integer
name = "John"

# Data type: string
```

**Operators:** Operators are symbols or keywords that perform operations on data. Common operators include addition (+), subtraction (-), multiplication (*), and division (/). They allow you to perform calculations and make decisions based on data values.

```java
// Arithmetic operators in Java
int result = 10 + 5; // Addition
int difference = 15 - 7; // Subtraction
int product = 6 * 4; // Multiplication
float quotient = 20 / 3.0; // Division
```

**Control Flow:** Programming languages provide control structures like conditionals (if-else statements), loops (for, while), and branching mechanisms to control the flow of a program. These constructs enable developers to create decision-making logic and execute code repeatedly.

```javascript
// Conditional statement in JavaScript
if (age >= 18) {
```

```
    console.log("You are an adult.");
} else {
    console.log("You are a minor.");
}
```

**Functions and Procedures:** Functions are reusable blocks of code that perform specific tasks. They encapsulate functionality and can accept input parameters and return values. Functions are essential for modularizing code and promoting code reusability.

```
// Function definition in C++
int add(int a, int b) {
    return a + b;
}
```

**Comments:** Comments are non-executable lines of code that provide explanations or annotations within the source code. They are essential for documenting code, making it more understandable for developers and maintainers.

```
# This is a single-line comment in Python

"""
This is a
multi-line comment
in Python.
"""
```

**Code Structure:** The structure of a program is determined by its organization into functions, classes, and modules. Well-structured code is easier to read, maintain, and debug. Code indentation and formatting conventions are often followed to enhance code readability.

Understanding these fundamental concepts is the first step in becoming proficient in any programming language. As we delve deeper into the specific languages discussed in this book, you'll see how these concepts are applied and extended to create diverse and powerful software solutions.

## 1.2 Evolution of Programming Languages

Programming languages have evolved significantly since the early days of computing. This evolution has been driven by the need for more expressive, efficient, and user-friendly tools for software development. In this section, we'll explore the historical development of programming languages, highlighting key milestones and innovations.

**Machine Language:** The earliest computers were programmed using machine language, which consisted of binary code instructions that directly controlled the hardware.

Programming in machine language was a tedious and error-prone process, as it required intimate knowledge of the computer's architecture.

**Assembly Language:** To simplify programming, assembly languages were introduced. These languages used symbolic names for machine-level instructions, making it somewhat easier for programmers to write code. However, assembly language was still closely tied to the underlying hardware.

```
MOV AL, 10   ; Move the value 10 into the AL register
ADD AL, 5    ; Add 5 to the AL register
```

**High-Level Languages:** High-level programming languages emerged in the mid-20th century, aiming to provide a more abstract and human-readable way of writing code. FORTRAN, developed in the late 1950s, was one of the first high-level languages and was designed for scientific and engineering calculations.

```
PROGRAM HelloWorld
  PRINT *, "Hello, World!"
END PROGRAM HelloWorld
```

**ALGOL:** In the late 1950s and early 1960s, ALGOL (Algorithmic Language) was developed, introducing structured programming concepts like loops and conditionals. ALGOL's influence can be seen in subsequent languages like Pascal and C.

**COBOL:** COBOL (Common Business-Oriented Language) was created in the early 1960s for business data processing. It introduced English-like syntax and was widely used in the business sector.

```
IDENTIFICATION DIVISION.
PROGRAM-ID. HelloWorld.
PROCEDURE DIVISION.
    DISPLAY "Hello, World!".
    STOP RUN.
```

**C Programming Language:** Developed in the early 1970s by Dennis Ritchie at Bell Labs, the C programming language was a major breakthrough. It provided low-level control, portability, and a simple syntax, making it popular for systems programming and later influencing many other languages.

```
#include <stdio.h>

int main() {
    printf("Hello, World!\n");
    return 0;
}
```

**Object-Oriented Programming (OOP):** The 1980s saw the emergence of OOP languages like C++ and Smalltalk, which introduced the concept of objects and classes for better code organization and modularity.

**Java:** In the mid-1990s, Java was introduced by Sun Microsystems. It emphasized portability and security by running on the Java Virtual Machine (JVM). Java's "Write Once, Run Anywhere" philosophy made it a popular choice for cross-platform development.

```
public class HelloWorld {
    public static void main(String[] args) {
        System.out.println("Hello, World!");
    }
}
```

**Scripting Languages:** Languages like Perl, Python, and Ruby gained popularity in the late 20th century for their ease of use and rapid development capabilities. They were particularly well-suited for web scripting and automation tasks.

The evolution of programming languages continues, with new languages constantly emerging to address specific needs and trends in the software development industry. Understanding this historical context is essential for appreciating the diverse landscape of programming languages available today.

## 1.3 Common Features of C, C++, Java, JavaScript, and Python

While there are countless programming languages in existence, each with its own unique features and use cases, some languages share common characteristics and principles. In this section, we'll explore the common features found in five widely used programming languages: C, C++, Java, JavaScript, and Python.

**1. Compiled vs. Interpreted:** C and C++ are compiled languages, meaning the source code is translated into machine code by a compiler before execution. This results in faster and more efficient programs but requires separate compilation for different platforms. In contrast, Java, JavaScript, and Python are interpreted languages. They are executed by an interpreter at runtime, allowing for greater portability but potentially sacrificing some performance.

**2. Syntax and Control Structures:** All five languages use C-style syntax, characterized by curly braces {} to denote code blocks and semicolons ; to terminate statements. They support common control structures like conditionals (if-else statements) and loops (for, while) for program flow control.

**3. Strong Typing:** C, C++, Java, JavaScript, and Python are all statically typed languages, meaning variable types are explicitly declared and checked at compile time. This helps catch type-related errors early in the development process, ensuring safer and more reliable code.

**4. Support for Functions/Methods:** Each language allows developers to define and use functions or methods. Functions in C and C++ are standalone, while Java, JavaScript, and Python support both standalone functions and methods within classes or objects.

**5. Libraries and Standard Libraries:** They all come with extensive standard libraries that provide pre-built functions and classes for common tasks. These libraries simplify development by offering a wealth of functionality, from file handling to networking.

**6. Memory Management:** C and C++ provide manual memory management, giving developers control over memory allocation and deallocation. Java, JavaScript, and Python, on the other hand, feature automatic memory management through garbage collection, simplifying memory-related tasks.

**7. Object-Oriented Programming (OOP):** C++, Java, and Python are object-oriented languages, promoting the use of classes and objects for modular and organized code. JavaScript, while not strictly OOP, supports object-based programming with its use of prototypes and object literals.

**8. Portability:** Java is known for its "Write Once, Run Anywhere" portability due to the Java Virtual Machine (JVM). JavaScript, being primarily used for web scripting, is highly portable across different browsers. Python is celebrated for its cross-platform compatibility, and C and C++ can be compiled for various platforms.

**9. Popular Use Cases:**

- C and C++ are favored for systems programming, game development, and applications where performance and low-level control are crucial.
- Java is commonly used in enterprise software, Android app development, and server-side applications.
- JavaScript is the language of the web, used for client-side scripting and building interactive web applications.
- Python excels in data science, machine learning, web development, scripting, and automation.

**10. Community and Ecosystem:** All these languages have active and thriving communities, which means ample resources, libraries, and frameworks are available for developers to leverage in their projects.

Understanding these common features can help developers make informed choices when selecting the most suitable programming language for their specific project requirements. Each language has its strengths and weaknesses, making them better suited for different tasks and domains.

---

## 1.4 High-Level vs. Low-Level Languages

Programming languages can be broadly categorized into two main groups: high-level languages and low-level languages. These categories refer to the level of abstraction and proximity to the hardware that a language operates at. In this section, we'll explore the distinctions between high-level and low-level languages and their respective advantages and trade-offs.

**High-Level Languages:**

High-level languages are designed with a focus on human readability and ease of programming. They offer a high level of abstraction, meaning that developers can write code that is closer to natural language and less concerned with the intricacies of the underlying hardware. Some key characteristics of high-level languages include:

1. **Abstraction:** High-level languages provide abstractions that simplify complex tasks. Developers can work with data structures, libraries, and functions that are closer to the problem domain they are addressing, rather than worrying about memory management or low-level operations.

2. **Portability:** Code written in high-level languages is generally more portable because it is less tied to specific hardware or operating systems. This makes it easier to write cross-platform software.

3. **Productivity:** High-level languages often enable faster development due to their concise syntax and rich set of built-in functions and libraries. Developers can focus on solving problems rather than dealing with low-level details.

4. **Readability:** High-level code is typically more readable and easier to understand for programmers, making it easier to maintain and collaborate on projects.

**Examples of High-Level Languages:**

- Python
- Java
- JavaScript
- Ruby
- Swift

**Low-Level Languages:**

Low-level languages, in contrast, provide minimal abstraction and are closer to the hardware. They allow for fine-grained control over a computer's resources but require more effort and attention to detail from the programmer. Key characteristics of low-level languages include:

1. **Control:** Low-level languages offer precise control over hardware resources such as memory and registers. This level of control is essential for systems programming and tasks where efficiency is critical.

2. **Performance:** Code written in low-level languages can be highly optimized for performance, as developers have direct control over memory allocation and CPU operations. This makes low-level languages suitable for tasks like writing operating systems or device drivers.

3.  **Hardware Dependence:** Programs written in low-level languages are often specific to a particular hardware architecture and operating system. Porting such code to different platforms can be challenging.

4.  **Complexity:** Writing code in low-level languages is generally more complex and error-prone due to the lack of high-level abstractions. Developers need to manage memory manually and handle many low-level details.

**Examples of Low-Level Languages:**

*   Assembly language
*   C
*   C++

**Choosing Between High-Level and Low-Level Languages:**

The choice between high-level and low-level languages depends on the specific requirements of a project. High-level languages are well-suited for most software development tasks, including web development, data analysis, and application development, where productivity and portability are crucial.

On the other hand, low-level languages are preferred for tasks that demand maximum performance, such as embedded systems programming, real-time systems, and writing system-level software.

In practice, many modern software systems combine both high-level and low-level languages. High-level languages are used for the majority of the application code, while critical performance-critical sections may be implemented in low-level languages or through language extensions like C/C++ bindings in Python or Java's Native Interface (JNI).

Understanding the trade-offs between high-level and low-level languages allows developers to make informed decisions about which language to use for a given project, balancing ease of development with performance requirements.

---

## 1.5 The Role of a Compiler and Interpreter

In the world of programming languages, compilers and interpreters play crucial roles in transforming human-readable code into machine-executable instructions. These tools are fundamental to the execution of code written in programming languages. Let's delve into the roles of compilers and interpreters and how they differ.

**Compilers:**

A compiler is a tool that translates the entire source code of a program into an equivalent set of machine code instructions. This translation is performed in a one-time process called compilation. Once the source code is compiled, it generates an executable binary file that can be run independently. Some key characteristics of compilers include:

1. **Compilation:** The source code is transformed into machine code before execution. This results in faster execution since there is no need to re-translate the code each time it runs.

2. **Efficiency:** Compiled programs are typically more efficient in terms of runtime performance because the code is optimized during compilation. This makes compilers well-suited for performance-critical applications.

3. **Static Typing:** Compilers often enforce strict static typing, catching type-related errors at compile-time. This can lead to more robust and reliable code.

4. **Examples:** Languages like C, C++, and Rust are typically compiled languages. Here's a simple example of a C program:

```
#include <stdio.h>

int main() {
    printf("Hello, World!\n");
    return 0;
}
```

**Interpreters:**

An interpreter, on the other hand, processes the source code line by line or statement by statement, executing it directly without creating a separate compiled binary. Interpreters read the source code, parse it, and execute it on the fly. Key characteristics of interpreters include:

1. **Dynamic Execution:** Interpreters execute code dynamically, which means the source code can be modified and executed without recompilation. This flexibility is useful for rapid development and scripting.

2. **Portability:** Since interpreters don't generate machine code binaries, the same source code can often run on different platforms with the corresponding interpreter installed.

3. **Dynamic Typing:** Interpreted languages often use dynamic typing, allowing for more flexibility in variable type handling. Type-related errors may only surface during runtime.

4. **Examples:** Languages like Python, JavaScript, and Ruby are typically interpreted languages. Here's a simple example of Python code:

```
print("Hello, World!")
```

**Hybrid Approaches:**

Some languages, like Java, employ a hybrid approach. Java source code is first compiled into an intermediate bytecode by the Java compiler. This bytecode is then interpreted by the Java Virtual Machine (JVM) at runtime, providing a compromise between the benefits of compilation and interpretation.

**Choosing Between Compilation and Interpretation:**

The choice between compilation and interpretation depends on various factors, including the nature of the project, performance requirements, and development speed. Compiled languages are suitable for performance-critical applications, while interpreted languages are often preferred for prototyping, web scripting, and rapid development.

In summary, compilers and interpreters are essential tools in the world of programming languages, each with its strengths and trade-offs. The choice between them depends on the specific needs and goals of a programming project.

# Chapter 2: Decoding C: The Ancestor of Modern Languages

## 2.1 The Birth and Philosophy of C

The C programming language, often referred to as the "mother of all programming languages," has a rich history and a significant impact on the development of modern programming languages. Created by Dennis Ritchie at Bell Labs in the early 1970s, C was designed with a specific philosophy in mind, which has shaped its features and principles.

**Philosophy of C:**

C was developed with a set of fundamental principles and goals that continue to influence programming languages today:

1. **Portability:** C was designed to be highly portable, allowing code written in C to run on different hardware platforms with minimal modifications. This portability was achieved by abstracting hardware details and providing a standard set of data types.

2. **Efficiency:** C prioritizes runtime efficiency and provides low-level control over hardware resources. This makes it well-suited for systems programming, where performance is crucial.

3. **Minimalism:** C follows a philosophy of minimalism, providing a small set of simple and powerful features. It avoids unnecessary complexity and features, which contributes to its simplicity and ease of learning.

4. **Close to Hardware:** C provides features for direct memory manipulation, pointer arithmetic, and low-level control over hardware. This closeness to the hardware allows developers to write efficient code but also demands responsibility in managing memory and resources.

**Sample C Code:**

Here's a simple "Hello, World!" program in C:

```c
#include <stdio.h>

int main() {
    printf("Hello, World!\n");
    return 0;
}
```

In this code, we include the standard input/output library (<stdio.h>) and define a main function, which is the entry point of a C program. The printf function is used to print the message to the standard output.

**Influence on Modern Languages:**

C's philosophy and design principles have had a profound impact on the development of modern programming languages:

- **C++:** C++ was developed as an extension of C, adding object-oriented features while preserving C's low-level capabilities.
- **Objective-C:** This language combines C with object-oriented programming and was used in Apple's macOS and iOS development.
- **C#:** Developed by Microsoft, C# draws heavily from C++ and C, with a focus on simplicity and type safety.
- **Java:** Java shares C's portability goals and simplicity in syntax, making it accessible to a wide range of developers.
- **Python:** While Python is a high-level language, its design principles of simplicity and readability are inspired by C.

Understanding the birth and philosophy of C is essential for grasping the foundations of modern programming languages and appreciating the design decisions that have shaped the software development landscape.

---

## 2.2 Structure of a C Program

C programs have a distinct structure that includes various elements and conventions. Understanding this structure is crucial when working with C, as it dictates how code is organized and executed. In this section, we'll explore the essential components of a C program and their roles.

**1. Preprocessor Directives:** C programs often begin with preprocessor directives. These are instructions to the preprocessor, which is a program that processes the source code before actual compilation. Preprocessor directives start with the # symbol and include commands like #include for including header files and #define for defining macros.

```
#include <stdio.h>
#define MAX 100
```

**2. Function Declarations:** The main structure of a C program typically includes function declarations. A C program must have at least one function named main, which serves as the entry point of the program. Functions are declared with their return type, name, and parameters.

```
int add(int a, int b);
void printMessage();
```

**3. The main Function:** The main function is the starting point of a C program. It contains the program's executable code. The main function does not take any parameters in its basic form and returns an integer, which is often used as an exit code.

```c
int main() {
    // Program code goes here
    return 0; // Exit with status code 0
}
```

**4. Statements and Expressions:** Within the `main` function or other user-defined functions, you write statements and expressions to perform tasks. Statements are terminated with a semicolon, and expressions evaluate to values.

```c
int sum = add(5, 3); // Expression
printf("The sum is %d\n", sum); // Statement
```

**5. Function Definitions:** Functions declared earlier must be defined somewhere in the program. Function definitions include the actual implementation of the function, including its logic and behavior.

```c
int add(int a, int b) {
    return a + b;
}

void printMessage() {
    printf("Hello, World!\n");
}
```

**6. Standard Input/Output:** C programs often use the standard input and output functions provided by the `<stdio.h>` library. These functions, like `printf` and `scanf`, enable interaction with the user through the console.

```c
#include <stdio.h>

int main() {
    int num;
    printf("Enter a number: ");
    scanf("%d", &num);
    printf("You entered: %d\n", num);
    return 0;
}
```

**7. Comments:** Comments in C are used to annotate code for documentation or explanation purposes. Single-line comments begin with //, and multi-line comments are enclosed between /* and */.

```c
// This is a single-line comment

/*
   This is a multi-line comment
   spanning multiple lines.
*/
```

**8. Variables and Data Types:** C supports various data types like `int`, `float`, `char`, and user-defined structures. Variables are declared with their data type, and they hold values during program execution.

```
int age = 25;
float price = 12.99;
char grade = 'A';
```

Understanding the structure of a C program is fundamental for writing and reading C code. As programs become more complex, maintaining a clear and organized structure becomes increasingly important for code readability and maintainability.

---

## 2.3 Memory Management in C

Memory management is a critical aspect of programming in C, as it provides control over the allocation and deallocation of memory resources. C allows for both static and dynamic memory management, giving developers flexibility but also requiring responsibility in managing memory efficiently. In this section, we'll explore memory management in C and its various aspects.

### 1. Static Memory Allocation:

In C, you can allocate memory for variables and arrays at compile-time, which is known as static memory allocation. Memory for these variables is allocated on the stack or in the data segment of the program.

```
int age; // Static memory allocation for an integer
```

### 2. Dynamic Memory Allocation:

Dynamic memory allocation in C is achieved using functions like `malloc`, `calloc`, and `realloc` from the `<stdlib.h>` library. This allows you to allocate memory at runtime and is particularly useful for creating data structures like arrays and linked lists.

```
int *numbers; // Declare a pointer
numbers = (int *)malloc(5 * sizeof(int)); // Dynamic memory allocation
```

### 3. Memory Deallocation:

When you allocate memory dynamically, it's essential to release that memory when it's no longer needed to prevent memory leaks. The `free` function is used to deallocate memory previously allocated with `malloc`, `calloc`, or `realloc`.

```
free(numbers); // Deallocate dynamically allocated memory
```

### 4. Pointers and Memory Access:

Pointers are a fundamental concept in C, allowing you to access and manipulate memory directly. However, improper use of pointers can lead to memory-related issues like segmentation faults and memory leaks.

```
int *ptr; // Declare a pointer
int value = 42;
ptr = &value; // Assign the address of 'value' to 'ptr'
```

## 5. Stack vs. Heap:

In C, memory can be allocated on the stack or the heap. Stack memory is automatically managed and is used for function call frames and local variables. Heap memory is explicitly managed and is suitable for dynamically allocated data.

## 6. Memory Safety:

C does not provide built-in memory safety features like bounds checking, which means developers must be cautious to avoid buffer overflows and other memory-related errors.

## 7. Memory Leaks:

A memory leak occurs when dynamically allocated memory is not properly deallocated. Detecting and fixing memory leaks is essential for maintaining a stable and efficient program.

## 8. Memory Alignment:

Memory alignment ensures that data is stored in memory at addresses that are multiples of specific values. Proper alignment can improve memory access speed and efficiency.

```
struct Data {
    int x;
    double y;
};

int main() {
    struct Data data; // Properly aligned structure
    // ...
    return 0;
}
```

## 9. Memory Management Best Practices:

To ensure efficient and safe memory management in C, consider the following best practices:

- Always deallocate dynamically allocated memory when it's no longer needed.
- Be mindful of buffer sizes and array bounds to prevent buffer overflows.
- Use pointers responsibly to avoid memory-related errors.
- Consider using data structures like linked lists and arrays to manage dynamic memory efficiently.

Memory management in C requires a deep understanding of the language's memory model and careful coding practices. While it provides fine-grained control over memory, it also demands responsibility from developers to avoid common pitfalls and issues related to memory allocation and deallocation.

## 2.4 C's Contribution to Operating Systems and Software

The C programming language has played a pivotal role in the development of operating systems and a wide range of software applications. Its combination of low-level control and portability has made it a preferred choice for building robust and efficient systems. In this section, we'll explore how C has contributed to the creation of operating systems and various software domains.

**1. Operating Systems:**

C's close-to-hardware capabilities and portability have made it an ideal language for developing operating systems (OS). Some of the most renowned operating systems, including Unix, Linux, and the Windows NT kernel, are primarily written in C. C's ability to manage hardware resources efficiently and provide a high degree of control is crucial for OS development.

**2. System Software:**

Beyond operating systems, C is extensively used in developing system software, such as device drivers, compilers, assemblers, and linkers. System software interfaces directly with hardware and needs to be both efficient and portable, making C an excellent choice.

```c
#include <stdio.h>

int main() {
    printf("Hello, System Software!\n");
    return 0;
}
```

**3. Embedded Systems:**

C's efficiency and low-level control make it suitable for embedded systems development. Embedded systems are found in various applications, including automotive control units, medical devices, and consumer electronics.

```c
void controlMotor(int speed) {
    // Control motor speed in an embedded system
}
```

**4. Networking Software:**

Networking software, including network protocols and servers, often relies on C for its performance and portability. C's socket programming libraries allow developers to create network applications that run efficiently across different platforms.

```c
#include <stdio.h>
#include <stdlib.h>
#include <sys/socket.h>
#include <netinet/in.h>

int main() {
    // Networking code here
    return 0;
}
```

## 5. Compilers and Interpreters:

C has a self-hosting nature, meaning that C compilers and interpreters are often written in C itself. This bootstrap process has led to the creation of many C compilers, such as GCC (GNU Compiler Collection) and Clang.

```c
int main() {
    printf("This program was compiled by a C compiler written in C!\n");
    return 0;
}
```

## 6. Scientific Computing:

C is employed in scientific computing for its computational efficiency. Libraries like BLAS (Basic Linear Algebra Subprograms) and LAPACK (Linear Algebra Package) are written in C and provide essential functions for numerical computations.

```c
#include <stdio.h>
#include <math.h>

int main() {
    double result = sqrt(25.0); // Square root calculation
    printf("The square root of 25 is %f\n", result);
    return 0;
}
```

## 7. Game Development:

C and C++ are popular choices for developing video games due to their performance capabilities. Game engines like Unreal Engine and Unity use C++ extensively, while game logic often utilizes C.

```c
#include <stdio.h>

int main() {
    // Game code here
```

```
    return 0;
}
```

## 8. Cross-Platform Development:

C's portability allows for cross-platform development, enabling software to run on different operating systems and architectures with minimal modifications.

The influence of C extends to various other domains, including database systems, security tools, and embedded control systems. Its longevity and adaptability have made it a cornerstone of modern software development, leaving a lasting impact on the technology landscape. Understanding C's contributions to these domains is essential for appreciating its continued relevance and importance in the field of computer science.

## 2.5 Limitations and Legacy of C

While C has been a groundbreaking and influential programming language, it is not without its limitations and challenges. In this section, we will explore some of the limitations of C and discuss its enduring legacy in the world of software development.

**1. Lack of Memory Safety:** C's low-level nature gives developers direct control over memory, but it also means there are no built-in safeguards against common memory-related errors like buffer overflows, null pointer dereferences, and memory leaks. Programmers must be diligent in managing memory to avoid these issues.

```
char buffer[10];
strcpy(buffer, "This is a long string that can overflow the buffer.");
```

**2. Portability Challenges:** While C is known for its portability, writing truly platform-independent code can still be challenging. Differences in hardware architectures, compilers, and operating systems can introduce subtle issues.

**3. Limited Standard Library:** C's standard library provides fundamental functionality, but it lacks the extensive libraries found in modern languages like Python or Java. Developers often need to rely on third-party libraries for more specialized tasks.

**4. Verbosity:** C can be verbose compared to modern high-level languages. For example, string manipulation or dynamic memory allocation can require more lines of code and be error-prone.

```
// Concatenate two strings in C
char str1[20] = "Hello, ";
char str2[10] = "world!";
strcat(str1, str2);
```

**5. Lack of Object-Oriented Features:** C does not provide native support for object-oriented programming (OOP) concepts like classes and inheritance, making it less suitable for large-scale software projects that benefit from OOP principles.

**6. Limited Concurrency Support:** C lacks built-in support for modern concurrency and parallelism. While it's possible to implement multithreading and multiprocessing, it can be complex and error-prone.

**7. Complexity in Error Handling:** Error handling in C often involves checking return values or error codes, which can lead to code clutter and decreased readability.

```
FILE *file = fopen("example.txt", "r");
if (file == NULL) {
    perror("Error opening file");
    return 1;
}
```

**8. Legacy Codebase Maintenance:** Legacy C codebases can be challenging to maintain and extend due to the absence of modern programming constructs. Refactoring or adding new features may require significant effort.

Despite these limitations, C's legacy in the world of software development remains strong. It continues to be a foundational language and serves as the basis for many other programming languages, including C++, Objective-C, and Rust. C's low-level control and efficiency make it indispensable in areas such as embedded systems, operating system development, and systems programming.

Moreover, C's limitations have inspired the development of safer and more modern languages that address these issues. For example, Rust focuses on memory safety and concurrency without sacrificing performance, while C++ introduces object-oriented features on top of C's foundations.

In conclusion, C's limitations are balanced by its enduring legacy and contributions to the field of programming. Its importance in the history of software development cannot be understated, and its principles continue to influence the design of new languages and systems. Understanding both its strengths and weaknesses is essential for developers working in a variety of software domains.

# Chapter 3: C++: Bridging Procedural and Object-Oriented Programming

## 3.1 The Evolution from C to C++

The development of C++ marked a significant evolution in programming languages, bridging the gap between procedural and object-oriented programming (OOP). In this section, we'll explore the journey from C to C++ and the core concepts that define C++ as a versatile and powerful language.

**1. Origins of C++:**

C++ was created by Bjarne Stroustrup in the early 1980s as an extension of the C programming language. Stroustrup's goal was to combine C's efficiency and low-level capabilities with high-level features, enabling more structured and modular code.

```cpp
#include <iostream>

int main() {
    std::cout << "Hello, C++!" << std::endl;
    return 0;
}
```

**2. Object-Oriented Programming (OOP):**

One of the fundamental shifts in C++ compared to C is the introduction of OOP. In C++, you can define classes and objects, encapsulating data and behavior into reusable and organized units.

```cpp
class Rectangle {
public:
    int width;
    int height;

    int area() {
        return width * height;
    }
};

int main() {
    Rectangle rect;
    rect.width = 5;
    rect.height = 10;

    int area = rect.area();
    return 0;
}
```

## 3. Classes and Objects:

Classes in C++ serve as blueprints for creating objects. They encapsulate data (attributes) and functions (methods) that operate on that data. Objects are instances of classes.

## 4. Inheritance:

C++ supports inheritance, allowing you to create new classes based on existing ones. Inheritance enables code reuse and the creation of class hierarchies.

```cpp
class Square : public Rectangle {
public:
    Square(int side) {
        width = side;
        height = side;
    }
};
```

## 5. Polymorphism:

Polymorphism in C++ allows objects of different classes to be treated as objects of a common base class. This facilitates dynamic method invocation and runtime flexibility.

```cpp
class Shape {
public:
    virtual void draw() {
        // Default implementation
    }
};

class Circle : public Shape {
public:
    void draw() override {
        // Draw a circle
    }
};
```

## 6. Encapsulation:

C++ supports encapsulation, hiding the internal details of a class and exposing only what's necessary. Access specifiers like public, private, and protected control the visibility of class members.

```cpp
class BankAccount {
private:
    double balance;

public:
    void deposit(double amount) {
        if (amount > 0) {
            balance += amount;
```

```
        }
    }

    double getBalance() {
        return balance;
    }
};
```

## 7. Templates:

C++ introduced templates, enabling generic programming. Templates allow you to write code that works with different data types while maintaining type safety.

```
template <typename T>
T add(T a, T b) {
    return a + b;
}
```

## 8. Standard Template Library (STL):

The STL is a collection of pre-defined classes and functions in C++ for common data structures (like vectors, lists, and maps) and algorithms. It simplifies complex tasks and promotes code reusability.

```
#include <vector>
#include <algorithm>

int main() {
    std::vector<int> numbers = {5, 2, 8, 1, 9};
    std::sort(numbers.begin(), numbers.end());
    return 0;
}
```

The evolution from C to C++ brought about a rich set of features and programming paradigms, making C++ a versatile language suitable for various applications. Its ability to seamlessly combine procedural and object-oriented programming has contributed to its enduring popularity in software development. Understanding C++'s core concepts is essential for leveraging its full potential in modern programming.

---

## 3.2 Core Concepts of Object-Oriented Programming in C++

Object-Oriented Programming (OOP) is a fundamental paradigm in C++, enabling developers to create more organized, modular, and maintainable code. In this section, we'll delve into the core concepts of OOP as applied in C++.

## 1. Classes and Objects:

At the heart of OOP in C++ are classes and objects. A class is a blueprint for creating objects. It defines attributes (data members) and methods (functions) that describe the behavior and properties of objects.

```cpp
class Circle {
public:
    double radius;

    double calculateArea() {
        return 3.14159 * radius * radius;
    }
};
```

In this example, Circle is a class with a radius attribute and a method calculateArea() that computes the area of a circle.

## 2. Encapsulation:

Encapsulation is the practice of bundling data (attributes) and the methods (functions) that operate on that data within a class. In C++, you can control the visibility of class members using access specifiers: public, private, and protected.

```cpp
class BankAccount {
private:
    double balance;

public:
    void deposit(double amount) {
        if (amount > 0) {
            balance += amount;
        }
    }

    double getBalance() {
        return balance;
    }
};
```

Here, the balance attribute is encapsulated as private, meaning it can only be accessed and modified through the public methods deposit() and getBalance().

## 3. Inheritance:

Inheritance allows you to create new classes (derived or subclass) based on existing ones (base or superclass). Derived classes inherit the attributes and methods of the base class, promoting code reuse and hierarchy.

```cpp
class Shape {
public:
    virtual double calculateArea() {
        return 0.0; // Default implementation
```

```
    }
};

class Circle : public Shape {
public:
    double radius;

    double calculateArea() override {
        return 3.14159 * radius * radius;
    }
};
```

In this example, `Circle` is a derived class of `Shape` and overrides the `calculateArea()` method to provide its own implementation.

**4. Polymorphism:**

Polymorphism allows objects of different classes to be treated as objects of a common base class. This facilitates dynamic method invocation and runtime flexibility.

```
Shape* shape = new Circle();
double area = shape->calculateArea();
```

Here, a `Circle` object is treated as a `Shape` object, and the `calculateArea()` method is called accordingly.

**5. Abstraction:**

Abstraction is the process of simplifying complex systems by modeling them as objects with specific behaviors and attributes. Classes provide a level of abstraction by encapsulating relevant details.

```
class Car {
public:
    virtual void start() = 0;
    virtual void stop() = 0;
};

class ElectricCar : public Car {
public:
    void start() override {
        // Start the electric car
    }

    void stop() override {
        // Stop the electric car
    }
};
```

In this example, `Car` is an abstract class with two pure virtual functions, enforcing that derived classes like `ElectricCar` must provide implementations for `start()` and `stop()`.

## 6. Composition:

Composition is the practice of building complex objects by combining simpler objects as attributes. It promotes code modularity and reusability.

```cpp
class Engine {
public:
    void start() {
        // Start the engine
    }

    void stop() {
        // Stop the engine
    }
};

class Car {
private:
    Engine engine;

public:
    void start() {
        engine.start();
    }

    void stop() {
        engine.stop();
    }
};
```

In this example, a Car contains an Engine as an attribute, allowing it to delegate tasks to the Engine object.

Understanding these core OOP concepts in C++ is essential for designing and developing software with a structured and modular approach. These concepts provide the foundation for building complex and maintainable systems, and they are widely used in a variety of applications, from game development to enterprise software.

---

## 3.3 Memory Management: From Malloc to Constructors

Memory management is a crucial aspect of C++ programming, and it differs significantly from C due to the introduction of classes and objects. In this section, we'll explore how C++ manages memory, including the use of constructors and destructors.

### 1. Constructors:

In C++, constructors are special member functions defined within a class that are called when an object of the class is created. Constructors initialize the object's attributes and allocate resources if necessary.

```cpp
class Student {
public:
    Student() {
        // Constructor
        age = 0;
        name = "Unknown";
    }

private:
    int age;
    std::string name;
};
```

In this example, the Student class has a constructor that sets default values for the age and name attributes when a Student object is created.

## 2. Destructor:

The destructor is another special member function that is called when an object goes out of scope or is explicitly deleted. Destructors are used to release resources allocated by the object, such as dynamic memory or file handles.

```cpp
class FileHandler {
public:
    FileHandler(const std::string& filename) {
        // Constructor: Open the file
        file.open(filename);
    }

    ~FileHandler() {
        // Destructor: Close the file
        file.close();
    }

private:
    std::ifstream file;
};
```

In this example, the FileHandler class has a constructor that opens a file and a destructor that closes the file when the object is destroyed.

## 3. Dynamic Memory Allocation:

C++ provides operators like new and delete for dynamic memory allocation and deallocation. When you use new to create an object, its constructor is called, and memory is allocated on the heap.

```cpp
Student* studentPtr = new Student(); // Dynamic object creation
```

To deallocate the memory and call the destructor, you use `delete`:

```cpp
delete studentPtr; // Destructor is called, and memory is freed
```

## 4. RAII (Resource Acquisition Is Initialization):

RAII is a C++ programming idiom that ties the lifetime of a resource (like memory or file handles) to the lifetime of an object. Constructors acquire resources, and destructors release them, ensuring that resources are properly managed.

```cpp
class DatabaseConnection {
public:
    DatabaseConnection() {
        // Constructor: Open a database connection
    }

    ~DatabaseConnection() {
        // Destructor: Close the database connection
    }
};
```

With RAII, resource management becomes automatic and deterministic, minimizing the risk of resource leaks.

## 5. Copy Constructors:

C++ provides copy constructors, which are used to create a copy of an existing object. By default, C++ generates a copy constructor that performs a member-wise copy. However, you can define a custom copy constructor to ensure proper copying of resources.

```cpp
class MyString {
public:
    MyString(const MyString& other) {
        // Custom copy constructor
        data = new char[strlen(other.data) + 1];
        strcpy(data, other.data);
    }

private:
    char* data;
};
```

In this example, the `MyString` class defines a custom copy constructor to create a deep copy of the character data.

Understanding memory management in C++ is essential for creating robust and resource-efficient programs. Constructors and destructors play a pivotal role in managing resources, and the RAII idiom encourages best practices in resource management. By using these features effectively, C++ developers can ensure proper allocation and deallocation of memory and other resources throughout the lifetime of objects.

---

## 3.4 The Standard Template Library (STL)

The Standard Template Library (STL) is a core component of C++ that provides a collection of pre-defined classes and functions for common data structures and algorithms. It simplifies complex tasks and promotes code reusability by offering a set of well-tested and efficient components. In this section, we'll explore some of the key components of the STL.

### 1. Containers:

STL provides several container classes for storing and managing data efficiently. Some commonly used containers include:

- **Vector:** A dynamic array that automatically resizes itself when elements are added or removed.
- **List:** A doubly-linked list that allows efficient insertion and deletion of elements anywhere in the list.
- **Map:** An associative container that stores key-value pairs, providing fast lookups by key.
- **Set:** A container that stores unique elements, useful for maintaining a collection of distinct values.

```
#include <vector>
#include <map>

std::vector<int> numbers = {1, 2, 3, 4, 5};
std::map<std::string, int> ageMap;
```

### 2. Iterators:

Iterators are used to traverse and manipulate elements in containers. They provide a uniform way to access elements regardless of the underlying container type.

```
for (auto it = numbers.begin(); it != numbers.end(); ++it) {
    // Access or modify elements using 'it'
}
```

### 3. Algorithms:

STL includes a wide range of algorithms that operate on containers. These algorithms perform tasks like sorting, searching, and modifying elements. Some commonly used algorithms include:

- **std::sort:** Sorts elements in a container.
- **std::find:** Searches for an element in a container.

- **std::for_each:** Applies a function to each element in a container.

```
#include <algorithm>

std::sort(numbers.begin(), numbers.end());
auto result = std::find(numbers.begin(), numbers.end(), 3);
```

## 4. Function Objects (Functors):

Functors are objects that behave like functions. They are often used with algorithms to customize their behavior. You can define your own functors by overloading the operator().

```
struct Square {
    int operator()(int x) const {
        return x * x;
    }
};

std::transform(numbers.begin(), numbers.end(), numbers.begin(), Square());
```

## 5. Strings:

C++ provides the std::string class as part of the STL, offering a more user-friendly and versatile alternative to C-style character arrays. std::string handles memory management and provides various string manipulation functions.

```
#include <string>

std::string greeting = "Hello, World!";
```

## 6. Smart Pointers:

STL includes smart pointers like std::shared_ptr, std::unique_ptr, and std::weak_ptr to manage dynamic memory efficiently. These pointers automatically handle memory deallocation when the object is no longer needed, reducing the risk of memory leaks.

```
#include <memory>

std::shared_ptr<int> sharedPtr = std::make_shared<int>(42);
std::unique_ptr<double> uniquePtr = std::make_unique<double>(3.14);
```

## 7. Utility Functions:

STL provides utility functions like std::pair and std::tuple for handling pairs and tuples of values. These are commonly used in functions and algorithms that return multiple values.

```
#include <utility>

std::pair<int, std::string> person = std::make_pair(25, "Alice");
```

```
std::tuple<int, double, std::string> data = std::make_tuple(42, 3.14, "Hello"
);
```

The Standard Template Library is a powerful tool for C++ developers, offering a wide range of reusable components and algorithms that simplify common programming tasks. By leveraging the STL effectively, programmers can write more efficient and maintainable code, reducing the need for reinventing the wheel when it comes to data structures and algorithms. Understanding the STL's components and how to use them is essential for any C++ developer.

## 3.5 Real-world Applications of C++

C++ is a versatile programming language known for its performance and efficiency. In this section, we'll explore some real-world applications of C++ and how it is used in various domains.

**1. Systems Programming:**

C++ is widely used for systems programming tasks. It plays a crucial role in developing operating systems, device drivers, and firmware for embedded systems. Its low-level capabilities make it suitable for managing hardware resources and interacting with peripherals.

```
// Example of systems programming in C++
#include <iostream>
#include <fstream>
#include <unistd.h>

int main() {
    std::cout << "Hello, C++ Systems Programming!" << std::endl;
    std::ofstream outputFile("data.txt");
    outputFile << "Data written to a file." << std::endl;
    close(1); // Close standard output
    return 0;
}
```

**2. Game Development:**

C++ is a popular choice for game development due to its performance and ability to handle resource-intensive tasks. Game engines like Unreal Engine and Unity use C++ extensively for their core systems.

```
// Game development in C++
#include <iostream>

class Game {
```

```cpp
public:
    void run() {
        // Game Loop
        while (isRunning) {
            // Game logic and rendering
        }
    }

private:
    bool isRunning = true;
};
```

### 3. High-Performance Computing (HPC):

C++ is favored in the field of high-performance computing, where maximum computational power is required. C++'s low-level memory control and optimization capabilities make it suitable for scientific simulations, weather modeling, and financial analysis.

```cpp
// High-performance computing in C++
#include <iostream>
#include <vector>
#include <omp.h>

int main() {
    std::vector<double> data(1000000, 0.0);

    #pragma omp parallel for
    for (int i = 0; i < data.size(); ++i) {
        data[i] = i * 2.0;
    }

    std::cout << "HPC task completed." << std::endl;
    return 0;
}
```

### 4. Aerospace and Defense:

C++ is used in the aerospace and defense industries for tasks like flight control systems, radar signal processing, and simulation software. Its reliability and real-time capabilities make it suitable for safety-critical applications.

```cpp
// Aerospace application in C++
#include <iostream>

class FlightControlSystem {
public:
    void controlFlight() {
        // Flight control logic
    }
};
```

## 5. Finance and Trading:

In the finance sector, C++ is used for algorithmic trading, risk management, and high-frequency trading systems. Its low-latency capabilities and efficient memory management are critical for processing large volumes of financial data.

```cpp
// Algorithmic trading in C++
#include <iostream>

class TradingAlgorithm {
public:
    void execute() {
        // Trading strategy implementation
    }
};
```

## 6. Game Engines and Graphics Libraries:

C++ is the language of choice for developing game engines and graphics libraries. Libraries like OpenGL and DirectX leverage C++'s performance to create immersive gaming experiences.

```cpp
// Graphics programming with C++
#include <iostream>
#include <OpenGL/gl.h>

int main() {
    // OpenGL rendering code
    return 0;
}
```

## 7. Automotive Industry:

C++ is used for developing embedded software in vehicles, including engine control units (ECUs), infotainment systems, and autonomous driving algorithms. Its real-time capabilities and performance are critical for automotive applications.

```cpp
// Automotive software development in C++
#include <iostream>

class AutonomousDrivingSystem {
public:
    void drive() {
        // Autonomous driving logic
    }
};
```

C++'s wide range of applications is a testament to its flexibility and power. It continues to be a preferred choice for projects that demand high performance, efficient memory management, and low-level control. Understanding how C++ is used across different domains is valuable for developers looking to specialize in specific industries or projects.

# Chapter 4: Java: Write Once, Run Anywhere

## 4.1 Java's Answer to Cross-Platform Compatibility

Java is renowned for its cross-platform compatibility, allowing developers to write code once and run it on multiple platforms without modification. In this section, we'll delve into Java's approach to achieving this portability and explore its core concepts.

### 1. The Java Virtual Machine (JVM):

At the heart of Java's platform independence is the JVM. Java source code is compiled into bytecode, which is executed by the JVM. This bytecode can run on any platform with a compatible JVM, ensuring that Java applications are platform-independent.

```
public class HelloWorld {
    public static void main(String[] args) {
        System.out.println("Hello, Java!");
    }
}
```

### 2. Write Once, Run Anywhere (WORA):

Java's WORA principle means that you can write Java code on one platform and run it on any platform with a compatible JVM. This eliminates the need to rewrite code for different operating systems.

### 3. Bytecode Compilation:

Java source code is compiled into bytecode by the Java compiler (`javac`). This bytecode is a platform-independent representation of the code and is saved in `.class` files.

```
javac HelloWorld.java
```

### 4. Platform-Specific JVMs:

While the JVM provides platform independence, there are different implementations of the JVM for various platforms. For example, Oracle provides the Oracle JVM, while OpenJDK offers an open-source alternative. These implementations ensure compatibility with specific operating systems.

### 5. Classpath and Jar Files:

Java applications can use external libraries and dependencies. These libraries are packaged in JAR (Java Archive) files. The classpath specifies the locations where the JVM should look for classes and JAR files.

```
java -cp .:mylibrary.jar MyApp
```

### 6. Platform-Dependent Libraries:

While Java code is portable, certain tasks may require platform-dependent code. In such cases, Java offers a mechanism called JNI (Java Native Interface) to interact with platform-specific libraries written in languages like C or C++.

```java
public class NativeLibraryExample {
    // Load a native library
    static {
        System.loadLibrary("myplatformlibrary");
    }

    // Declare a native method
    public native void platformSpecificMethod();
}
```

## 7. GUI and User Interface:

Java provides platform-independent libraries for creating graphical user interfaces (GUIs). Swing and JavaFX are examples of GUI libraries that allow developers to build cross-platform desktop applications.

```java
import javax.swing.*;

public class SimpleGUI {
    public static void main(String[] args) {
        SwingUtilities.invokeLater(() -> {
            JFrame frame = new JFrame("Hello, GUI!");
            frame.setDefaultCloseOperation(JFrame.EXIT_ON_CLOSE);
            frame.setSize(300, 200);
            frame.setVisible(true);
        });
    }
}
```

## 8. Web Applications:

Java is widely used for web development. Java-based web applications can run on any web server that supports Java Servlets. Technologies like Java EE (Enterprise Edition) provide tools for building scalable web applications.

```java
@WebServlet("/HelloServlet")
public class HelloServlet extends HttpServlet {
    protected void doGet(HttpServletRequest request, HttpServletResponse response) throws ServletException, IOException {
        response.getWriter().write("Hello, Web!");
    }
}
```

Java's promise of cross-platform compatibility has made it a popular choice for a wide range of applications. From desktop software to web and mobile apps, Java's ability to run on multiple platforms without modification has simplified software development and deployment. Understanding Java's key principles, like bytecode compilation and the JVM, is essential for harnessing its cross-platform capabilities effectively.

## 4.2 Understanding Java Virtual Machine (JVM)

The Java Virtual Machine (JVM) is a critical component of the Java platform, responsible for executing Java bytecode and ensuring cross-platform compatibility. In this section, we'll explore the JVM in-depth and understand its role in making Java a write-once-run-anywhere language.

### 1. JVM Architecture:

The JVM is a virtualized runtime environment that abstracts the underlying hardware and operating system. It consists of several components, including:

- **Class Loader:** Responsible for loading classes and interfaces at runtime.
- **Execution Engine:** Interprets and executes bytecode or compiles it to native code for improved performance.
- **Memory Area:** Divided into various segments like method area, heap, stack, and native method stack.
- **Java Native Interface (JNI):** Allows Java code to interact with platform-specific native libraries.
- **Native Method Interface (NMI):** Provides a bridge between the JVM and native libraries.

### 2. Bytecode Execution:

When a Java source code is compiled, it generates bytecode instructions, which are stored in .class files. These bytecode instructions are platform-independent and can be executed by any JVM.

```java
public class HelloWorld {
    public static void main(String[] args) {
        System.out.println("Hello, Java!");
    }
}
```

### 3. Just-In-Time (JIT) Compilation:

To improve performance, many JVM implementations use Just-In-Time (JIT) compilation. Instead of interpreting bytecode, the JIT compiler translates it into native machine code at runtime, allowing for faster execution.

### 4. Class Loading:

The class loader is responsible for loading classes into the JVM as they are needed. There are three main class loaders: the Bootstrap Class Loader, the Extension Class Loader, and the Application Class Loader. They work together to load classes from system libraries, extensions, and application code, respectively.

```
ClassLoader classLoader = MyClass.class.getClassLoader();
```

## 5. Memory Management:

The JVM manages memory using different segments, including the heap (for object storage), the method area (for class metadata), the stack (for method calls and local variables), and the native method stack (for native method calls).

```
int[] array = new int[1000]; // Memory allocated on the heap
```

## 6. Garbage Collection:

Java employs automatic garbage collection to reclaim memory occupied by objects that are no longer in use. The JVM periodically identifies and frees memory from unreachable objects.

```
// Explicitly trigger garbage collection
System.gc();
```

## 7. Java Native Interface (JNI):

JNI enables Java code to call functions written in languages like C and C++. It is used when platform-specific functionality is required or for integrating with existing native libraries.

```
public class NativeLibraryExample {
    // Load a native library
    static {
        System.loadLibrary("myplatformlibrary");
    }

    // Declare a native method
    public native void platformSpecificMethod();
}
```

## 8. Multithreading:

The JVM supports multithreading, allowing Java applications to execute multiple threads concurrently. Java's java.lang.Thread class and various synchronization mechanisms enable developers to create multi-threaded applications.

```
class MyThread extends Thread {
    public void run() {
        // Thread execution logic
    }
}
```

```
MyThread thread1 = new MyThread();
thread1.start(); // Start the thread
```

## 9. Security and Sandbox:

The JVM incorporates security features to create a safe execution environment. It enforces access controls, bytecode verification, and provides a security manager to restrict potentially harmful operations.

Understanding the JVM's inner workings is crucial for Java developers to optimize their code and troubleshoot issues effectively. It also enables developers to harness the full potential of Java's platform independence and write robust, cross-platform applications.

---

## 4.3 Object-Oriented Principles in Java

Java is renowned for its strong adherence to object-oriented programming (OOP) principles. In this section, we'll delve into the core concepts of OOP in Java and how they contribute to the language's design and structure.

## 1. Classes and Objects:

At the heart of Java's OOP paradigm are classes and objects. A class defines a blueprint for objects, specifying their attributes (fields) and behaviors (methods).

```
public class Student {
    // Fields
    String name;
    int age;

    // Constructor
    public Student(String name, int age) {
        this.name = name;
        this.age = age;
    }

    // Method
    public void study() {
        System.out.println(name + " is studying.");
    }
}
```

In this example, the Student class defines fields (name and age), a constructor to initialize objects, and a method (study) to perform an action.

## 2. Encapsulation:

Java encourages encapsulation, the practice of bundling data (fields) and methods that operate on that data within a single unit (class). This helps maintain data integrity and control access.

```java
public class BankAccount {
    private double balance;

    public void deposit(double amount) {
        // Deposit logic
        balance += amount;
    }

    public double getBalance() {
        return balance;
    }
}
```

The balance field is encapsulated within the BankAccount class, and access to it is controlled through methods like deposit and getBalance.

### 3. Inheritance:

Inheritance allows one class (subclass or derived class) to inherit the attributes and behaviors of another class (superclass or base class). Java supports single inheritance (a subclass can inherit from one superclass) and multiple interfaces (a class can implement multiple interfaces).

```java
public class Animal {
    void eat() {
        System.out.println("Animal is eating.");
    }
}
```

```java
public class Dog extends Animal {
    void bark() {
        System.out.println("Dog is barking.");
    }
}
```

In this example, the Dog class inherits the eat method from the Animal class.

### 4. Polymorphism:

Polymorphism allows objects of different classes to be treated as objects of a common superclass. It enables method overriding and dynamic method binding.

```java
class Shape {
    void draw() {
        System.out.println("Drawing a shape.");
    }
}
```

```java
class Circle extends Shape {
    @Override
    void draw() {
        System.out.println("Drawing a circle.");
    }
}

class Square extends Shape {
    @Override
    void draw() {
        System.out.println("Drawing a square.");
    }
}
```

Polymorphism allows you to treat objects of Circle and Square as Shape objects and call their draw methods without knowing their specific types.

### 5. Abstraction:

Abstraction is the process of simplifying complex reality by modeling classes based on essential attributes and behaviors. Abstract classes and interfaces are used to define abstractions in Java.

```java
abstract class Shape {
    abstract void draw();
}

class Circle extends Shape {
    @Override
    void draw() {
        System.out.println("Drawing a circle.");
    }
}
```

In this example, Shape is an abstract class with an abstract method draw. Subclasses like Circle provide concrete implementations.

### 6. Interfaces:

Java supports interfaces, which define a contract that classes must adhere to. A class can implement multiple interfaces, enabling multiple inheritance of behavior.

```java
interface Drawable {
    void draw();
}

class Circle implements Drawable {
    @Override
    void draw() {
        System.out.println("Drawing a circle.");
```

```
    }
}
```

Here, the `Circle` class implements the `Drawable` interface and provides an implementation of the `draw` method.

Java's strong OOP foundation makes it suitable for building modular, maintainable, and extensible software systems. Understanding and applying OOP principles like encapsulation, inheritance, polymorphism, and abstraction is essential for effective Java development.

## 4.4 Garbage Collection in Java

Java's automatic garbage collection (GC) is a fundamental feature that helps manage memory by reclaiming memory occupied by objects that are no longer referenced. In this section, we'll explore how garbage collection works in Java and its significance in preventing memory leaks.

**1. Memory Management in Java:**

In Java, developers allocate memory for objects using the new keyword. The JVM's memory management system divides memory into various areas, including the heap, method area, stack, and native method stack.

- **Heap:** The heap is where objects are allocated and deallocated. It's the main area managed by the garbage collector.
- **Method Area:** This area stores class metadata, static variables, and constant pool data.
- **Stack:** Each thread has its own stack, which contains method call frames and local variables.
- **Native Method Stack:** Used for native method calls.

**2. Reference Counting:**

In some programming languages, objects are tracked using reference counting, where each object keeps track of the number of references to it. When the reference count drops to zero, the object is considered no longer in use and can be deallocated.

```
class MyObject {
    int data;
    MyObject reference;

    MyObject(int data) {
        this.data = data;
    }
}
```

```java
MyObject obj1 = new MyObject(1);
MyObject obj2 = new MyObject(2);

obj1.reference = obj2;
obj2.reference = obj1;
```

However, Java does not use reference counting as its primary memory management technique because it cannot handle cyclic references efficiently.

### 3. Reachability Analysis:

Java employs reachability analysis to determine whether an object is still in use. An object is considered reachable if it can be accessed through references from the root set, which includes objects referenced by active threads, local variables, and static variables.

```java
public class ReachabilityExample {
    public static void main(String[] args) {
        MyObject obj1 = new MyObject(1);
        MyObject obj2 = new MyObject(2);

        obj1.reference = obj2;
        obj2.reference = obj1;

        // obj1 and obj2 are still reachable
    }
}
```

In this example, even though obj1 and obj2 reference each other, they are considered reachable because they can be accessed through the local variables obj1 and obj2.

### 4. The Role of the Garbage Collector:

The garbage collector's primary role is to identify and reclaim memory occupied by objects that are no longer reachable. It does this by periodically traversing the object graph from the root set and marking reachable objects. Unreachable objects are then deallocated, freeing up memory for future allocations.

### 5. Types of Garbage Collectors:

Java provides several garbage collection algorithms, each suited for specific scenarios. Common types include:

- **Serial Garbage Collector:** Suitable for single-threaded applications.
- **Parallel Garbage Collector:** Designed for multi-threaded applications with low pause time requirements.
- **Concurrent Mark-Sweep (CMS) Garbage Collector:** Reduces pause times for applications sensitive to latency.
- **G1 Garbage Collector:** Designed for large heaps and improved throughput with low pause times.

## 6. Explicit Garbage Collection:

While the JVM automatically manages memory, developers can request an explicit garbage collection using `System.gc()` or `Runtime.getRuntime().gc()`. However, it's generally discouraged, as the JVM is typically more efficient at determining when to run the GC.

```
System.gc(); // Explicitly request garbage collection
```

## 7. Memory Leaks:

A memory leak occurs when objects are unintentionally kept in memory because they are not properly dereferenced. Java's garbage collector helps prevent memory leaks by reclaiming memory from unreachable objects. However, developers should be cautious with long-lived references to objects to avoid unintentional memory retention.

Understanding how garbage collection works in Java is essential for writing efficient and memory-safe applications. Java's automatic memory management system helps simplify memory handling, but developers should still be aware of best practices to ensure optimal memory usage and avoid memory leaks.

---

## 4.5 Java in Enterprise Solutions

Java's versatility and robust features have made it a popular choice for developing enterprise-level applications and solutions. In this section, we'll explore why Java is well-suited for the enterprise and delve into some of its prominent use cases.

## 1. Platform Independence:

One of Java's key strengths in the enterprise is its platform independence. Java applications can run on various operating systems and hardware, making it easier to deploy and maintain software across diverse environments. This compatibility reduces the total cost of ownership for enterprises.

## 2. Scalability:

Java is highly scalable, allowing enterprises to build applications that can handle increasing workloads and adapt to growing user bases. Java's support for multithreading and distributed computing makes it suitable for large-scale systems.

## 3. Reliability and Stability:

Java is known for its stability and reliability. Enterprises rely on Java for mission-critical applications where system crashes or unexpected behavior are not acceptable. Java's memory management and exception handling contribute to its robustness.

## 4. Security:

Security is paramount in enterprise solutions, and Java offers several security features. It has a robust security model, including the use of a Security Manager to control untrusted code. Java regularly releases security updates to address vulnerabilities.

## 5. Enterprise Edition (Java EE):

Java EE, now known as Jakarta EE, is a set of specifications that extends the Java SE platform for building large-scale, distributed enterprise applications. It provides standardized APIs for tasks like database access, messaging, and web services.

```
@WebServlet("/HelloServlet")
public class HelloServlet extends HttpServlet {
    protected void doGet(HttpServletRequest request, HttpServletResponse resp
onse) throws ServletException, IOException {
        response.getWriter().write("Hello, Enterprise!");
    }
}
```

## 6. Web Applications:

Java is widely used in the development of web applications. Java Servlets and JavaServer Pages (JSP) are technologies commonly employed to build dynamic and interactive web applications. Frameworks like Spring and JavaServer Faces (JSF) facilitate web development.

## 7. Enterprise Integration:

Many enterprises operate with legacy systems and databases. Java provides libraries and tools for integrating with these systems, ensuring a smooth transition to modern solutions without disrupting existing operations.

## 8. Microservices Architecture:

Java is well-suited for microservices architecture, where applications are divided into small, independently deployable services. Containers like Docker and orchestration tools like Kubernetes are often used in conjunction with Java for managing microservices.

## 9. Big Data and Analytics:

Java has a presence in the big data and analytics domain. Apache Hadoop and Apache Spark, two widely-used big data frameworks, are primarily developed in Java. Java's performance and scalability are assets in processing large datasets.

## 10. DevOps and Continuous Integration:

Java integrates well with DevOps practices and continuous integration/continuous deployment (CI/CD) pipelines. Tools like Jenkins, Maven, and Gradle are commonly used for building, testing, and deploying Java applications.

## 11. Mobile and IoT Applications:

While Android primarily uses Java for mobile app development, Java's portability and suitability for embedded systems make it a viable choice for Internet of Things (IoT) applications.

## 12. Financial Services:

The financial industry heavily relies on Java for building trading platforms, risk management systems, and electronic trading solutions due to Java's low latency and high throughput capabilities.

## 13. Healthcare and Telecommunications:

Java is prevalent in healthcare systems, managing patient records and hospital operations. In the telecommunications sector, it's used for network management and communication protocols.

Java's presence in enterprise solutions continues to grow as organizations seek reliable, scalable, and secure technologies to power their operations. Its adaptability to various domains, along with a rich ecosystem of libraries and frameworks, makes Java a dependable choice for enterprises across industries.

# Chapter 5: JavaScript: The Language of the Web

## 5.1 From Simple Scripts to Rich Web Applications

JavaScript is a dynamic and versatile programming language that plays a pivotal role in modern web development. In this section, we'll explore JavaScript's journey from its origins as a simple scripting language to its current status as a powerful tool for building rich web applications.

### 1. A Brief History:

JavaScript was created by Brendan Eich in 1995 while he was working at Netscape Communications. Initially named "LiveScript," it was later renamed "JavaScript" to leverage the popularity of Java. JavaScript's early days were focused on enhancing the interactivity of web pages through client-side scripting.

```javascript
// An early JavaScript example
function greet(name) {
    return "Hello, " + name + "!";
}
```

### 2. DOM Manipulation:

One of JavaScript's initial use cases was manipulating the Document Object Model (DOM) to interact with web page elements dynamically. Developers could now change content, style, and behavior without requiring a full page reload.

```javascript
// Changing the text content of an HTML element
document.getElementById("greeting").textContent = "Welcome!";
```

### 3. Rise of AJAX:

In the early 2000s, JavaScript played a crucial role in the rise of Asynchronous JavaScript and XML (AJAX). This technology allowed web applications to fetch data from the server without reloading the entire page, leading to more responsive and interactive web experiences.

```javascript
// Making an AJAX request with XMLHttpRequest
var xhr = new XMLHttpRequest();
xhr.open("GET", "https://api.example.com/data", true);
xhr.onreadystatechange = function() {
    if (xhr.readyState === 4 && xhr.status === 200) {
        var data = JSON.parse(xhr.responseText);
        console.log(data);
    }
};
xhr.send();
```

### 4. The Birth of Libraries and Frameworks:

As web applications became more complex, JavaScript libraries and frameworks emerged to simplify development. jQuery, released in 2006, gained immense popularity for its DOM manipulation capabilities and cross-browser compatibility.

```javascript
// jQuery example: toggling a CSS class
$("#myButton").click(function() {
    $("#myElement").toggleClass("highlight");
});
```

## 5. Server-Side JavaScript with Node.js:

Node.js, introduced in 2009, brought JavaScript to the server-side, allowing developers to use a single language for both client and server applications. This unified approach led to significant advancements in full-stack development.

```javascript
// A simple Node.js server
const http = require("http");

const server = http.createServer((req, res) => {
    res.writeHead(200, { "Content-Type": "text/plain" });
    res.end("Hello, Node.js!");
});

server.listen(8080, "localhost");
```

## 6. Front-End Frameworks and Single-Page Applications (SPAs):

The emergence of front-end frameworks like Angular, React, and Vue.js transformed JavaScript into a key player in building SPAs. These frameworks offer component-based architecture and improved state management.

```javascript
// React component example
import React from "react";

function Greeting(props) {
    return <h1>Hello, {props.name}!</h1>;
}
```

## 7. The Modern Web Ecosystem:

Today, JavaScript is an integral part of the modern web ecosystem. It powers not only web applications but also mobile app development through technologies like React Native and progressive web apps (PWAs).

## 8. Beyond the Browser:

JavaScript's versatility extends beyond web development. It is used in robotics, IoT, serverless computing, and more, thanks to projects like Node.js and Electron.

```javascript
// Building a desktop application with Electron
const { app, BrowserWindow } = require("electron");
```

```
app.on("ready", () => {
    const mainWindow = new BrowserWindow({ width: 800, height: 600 });
    mainWindow.loadFile("index.html");
});
```

JavaScript has evolved from a simple scripting language to a powerful and ubiquitous tool in the world of web development and beyond. Its continuous growth and adaptability make it a compelling choice for developers looking to create dynamic and interactive applications.

## 5.2 Understanding the DOM and Browser Rendering

To work effectively with JavaScript in web development, it's crucial to understand the Document Object Model (DOM) and how the browser renders web pages. In this section, we'll explore the DOM and the rendering process, which are fundamental to JavaScript's role in enhancing web interactivity.

### 1. What Is the DOM?

The DOM is a programming interface for web documents. It represents the structure of a web page, allowing scripts (like JavaScript) to access and manipulate the content, structure, and style of a document. The DOM is a tree-like structure where each element in an HTML document is represented as a node, and elements are organized hierarchically.

```
<!DOCTYPE html>
<html>
<head>
    <title>DOM Example</title>
</head>
<body>
    <h1>Welcome to the DOM</h1>
    <p>This is a paragraph.</p>
</body>
</html>
```

In this HTML example, the DOM representation would consist of nodes like <html>, <head>, <title>, <body>, <h1>, and <p>.

### 2. How JavaScript Interacts with the DOM:

JavaScript can interact with the DOM through a set of APIs provided by the browser. These APIs allow you to:

- Access and manipulate HTML elements.
- Change element attributes and content.

- Add or remove elements.
- Respond to user events like clicks and keypresses.

Here's a simple example of how JavaScript can change the text of an HTML element:

```javascript
// Get the element with the ID "myElement"
var element = document.getElementById("myElement");

// Change its text content
element.textContent = "New Text";
```

### 3. Browser Rendering Process:

Understanding how the browser renders a web page is essential when working with JavaScript. The rendering process involves several steps:

a. **Parsing HTML:** The browser parses the HTML document to create a DOM tree.

b. **Constructing the Render Tree:** The browser combines the DOM tree with the CSSOM (CSS Object Model) to create a render tree, which represents what should be displayed on the screen.

c. **Layout:** The browser calculates the layout of each element, determining their size and position on the screen.

d. **Painting:** Finally, the browser paints the elements on the screen according to their layout information.

### 4. Efficient DOM Manipulation:

Efficiency is crucial when working with the DOM. Excessive DOM manipulation can lead to performance issues, especially on large web pages. To optimize DOM manipulation:

- Minimize direct DOM access and manipulation in loops.
- Use event delegation to handle events efficiently on parent elements.
- Cache DOM references for elements you frequently interact with.
- Use libraries like jQuery or modern frameworks to simplify DOM manipulation.

### 5. Asynchronous JavaScript:

JavaScript's asynchronous nature is fundamental for web interactivity. Functions like setTimeout and addEventListener allow you to schedule code execution and respond to user interactions without blocking the main thread, ensuring a smooth user experience.

```javascript
// Execute a function after a delay
setTimeout(function() {
    console.log("Delayed code execution");
}, 2000);
```

Understanding the DOM and the browser rendering process is crucial for effective web development with JavaScript. By manipulating the DOM and optimizing your code, you can create dynamic and interactive web applications that provide a seamless user experience.

## 5.3 Event-Driven Programming in JavaScript

Event-driven programming is a core concept in JavaScript, allowing developers to create interactive and responsive web applications. In this section, we'll delve into event-driven programming in JavaScript, explaining how events work, how to handle them, and their significance in modern web development.

### 1. Understanding Events:

In JavaScript, an event is an action or occurrence that can be detected and responded to by code. Examples of events include user interactions like clicks, keyboard input, mouse movements, and window resizing. Events are generated by various sources, including the user, the browser, or external devices.

```
// Adding a click event listener to a button element
var button = document.getElementById("myButton");
button.addEventListener("click", function() {
    console.log("Button clicked!");
});
```

In this example, we attach a click event listener to a button element. When the button is clicked, the provided function is executed.

### 2. Event Handling:

Event handling in JavaScript involves:

- Registering an event listener on an HTML element.
- Specifying the event type (e.g., "click," "keydown").
- Providing a callback function that executes when the event occurs.

```
// Handling a keyboard event
document.addEventListener("keydown", function(event) {
    console.log("Key pressed: " + event.key);
});
```

Here, we register a keydown event listener on the entire document. When a key is pressed, the callback function logs the pressed key to the console.

### 3. Event Propagation:

Events in the DOM follow a propagation model that includes two phases: capturing phase and bubbling phase. The capturing phase starts from the root and moves down to the

64

target element, while the bubbling phase starts from the target element and moves up to the root.

```javascript
// Event propagation example
var container = document.getElementById("container");
var button = document.getElementById("myButton");

container.addEventListener("click", function() {
    console.log("Container clicked");
}, true); // Capturing phase

button.addEventListener("click", function() {
    console.log("Button clicked");
}); // Bubbling phase
```

In this example, when the button is clicked, both the container and button's click event handlers are triggered. The capturing phase handler runs first, followed by the bubbling phase handler.

### 4. Preventing Default Behavior:

Many DOM events have default behaviors associated with them. For instance, clicking on a link navigates to a new page by default. JavaScript allows you to prevent the default behavior of an event when needed.

```javascript
// Preventing the default behavior of a link
var link = document.getElementById("myLink");
link.addEventListener("click", function(event) {
    event.preventDefault();
    console.log("Link click prevented");
});
```

In this example, clicking the link prevents the default navigation behavior, and the event's propagation is halted.

### 5. Event Delegation:

Event delegation is a technique where a single event listener is attached to a parent element to handle events for multiple child elements. This is especially useful when dealing with dynamically generated content.

```javascript
// Event delegation example
var container = document.getElementById("container");

container.addEventListener("click", function(event) {
    if (event.target.tagName === "LI") {
        console.log("List item clicked");
    }
});
```

In this example, we listen for clicks on a container element and check if the clicked element is an `<li>` (list item). This allows us to handle clicks on multiple list items with a single event listener.

### 6. Asynchronous Event Handling:

JavaScript's asynchronous nature is well-suited for event-driven programming. Events can be used to trigger asynchronous operations, such as making AJAX requests, updating UI elements, or handling user interactions without blocking the main thread.

Event-driven programming is at the heart of modern web development. JavaScript's ability to respond to user actions and external events enables the creation of dynamic and interactive web applications. Understanding event handling and propagation is essential for building responsive and user-friendly interfaces in the browser.

---

## 5.4 Asynchronous Programming and Callbacks

Asynchronous programming is a critical aspect of JavaScript, allowing developers to perform tasks without blocking the main thread, ensuring a responsive user interface. Callback functions are fundamental to handling asynchronous operations. In this section, we'll explore asynchronous programming using callbacks in JavaScript.

### 1. Asynchronous Operations:

JavaScript frequently encounters tasks that take time to complete, such as fetching data from a server or reading a file. Performing these tasks synchronously would freeze the user interface, making the application unresponsive. Asynchronous programming addresses this issue by allowing tasks to run in the background.

### 2. Callback Functions:

Callbacks are functions passed as arguments to other functions. They are executed once a specific task is completed. Callbacks are commonly used to handle asynchronous operations in JavaScript.

```javascript
// Example of a callback function
function fetchData(url, callback) {
    // Simulate fetching data
    setTimeout(function() {
        var data = "Data fetched from " + url;
        callback(data);
    }, 1000);
}

// Using the callback
fetchData("https://example.com/api/data", function(result) {
```

```
    console.log(result);
});
```

In this example, the `fetchData` function simulates data fetching and executes the provided callback function when the data is ready.

### 3. Callback Hell (Pyramid of Doom):

Callback functions can lead to a problem known as "Callback Hell" or the "Pyramid of Doom" when dealing with multiple nested asynchronous operations. This can result in code that is difficult to read and maintain.

```
// Example of callback hell
asyncFunc1(function(result1) {
    asyncFunc2(result1, function(result2) {
        asyncFunc3(result2, function(result3) {
            // More nested callbacks...
        });
    });
});
```

### 4. Promises:

To mitigate the issue of callback hell, JavaScript introduced Promises. A Promise represents a value that may not be available yet but will be at some point in the future. Promises provide a cleaner way to handle asynchronous operations.

```
// Example using Promises
function fetchData(url) {
    return new Promise(function(resolve, reject) {
        setTimeout(function() {
            var data = "Data fetched from " + url;
            resolve(data); // Resolve the Promise with data
        }, 1000);
    });
}
```

```
// Using Promises
fetchData("https://example.com/api/data")
    .then(function(result) {
        console.log(result);
    })
    .catch(function(error) {
        console.error(error);
    });
```

Promises allow you to chain `.then()` handlers for success and `.catch()` handlers for errors, making the code more readable and maintainable.

### 5. Async/Await:

ES2017 introduced the async and await keywords, which further simplify asynchronous code. An async function returns a Promise, and await can be used inside it to pause execution until the awaited Promise is resolved.

```
// Example using async/await
async function fetchData(url) {
    return new Promise(function(resolve, reject) {
        setTimeout(function() {
            var data = "Data fetched from " + url;
            resolve(data); // Resolve the Promise with data
        }, 1000);
    });
}

// Using async/await
async function getData() {
    try {
        const result = await fetchData("https://example.com/api/data");
        console.log(result);
    } catch (error) {
        console.error(error);
    }
}

getData();
```

Async/await syntax makes asynchronous code appear more like synchronous code, improving readability.

Understanding asynchronous programming and callback functions is crucial for building responsive and efficient JavaScript applications. While callbacks are a fundamental concept, Promises and async/await have become standard practices for managing asynchronous operations and reducing callback hell.

---

## 5.5 The Rise of Node.js and Server-Side JavaScript

Node.js has emerged as a game-changer in the world of server-side development, allowing JavaScript to extend its reach beyond the browser. In this section, we'll explore the rise of Node.js, its architecture, and its significance in modern web development.

**1. Introduction to Node.js:**

Node.js, initially released in 2009 by Ryan Dahl, is an open-source, cross-platform runtime environment that allows developers to run JavaScript on the server-side. It leverages Google's V8 JavaScript engine for fast code execution and provides a rich set of built-in libraries and modules for server-side tasks.

```
// A simple HTTP server using Node.js
const http = require('http');

const server = http.createServer((req, res) => {
  res.statusCode = 200;
  res.setHeader('Content-Type', 'text/plain');
  res.end('Hello, Node.js!');
});

server.listen(8080, 'localhost', () => {
  console.log('Server running at http://localhost:8080/');
});
```

**2. Event-Driven and Non-Blocking Architecture:**

Node.js follows an event-driven, non-blocking I/O model, making it highly efficient for handling concurrent connections. This architecture allows Node.js to process multiple requests simultaneously without the need for thread-based concurrency. Instead, it relies on callbacks and event loops for asynchronous operations.

```
// Asynchronous file read in Node.js
const fs = require('fs');

fs.readFile('file.txt', 'utf8', (err, data) => {
  if (err) throw err;
  console.log(data);
});
```

**3. npm (Node Package Manager):**

npm is the package manager for Node.js, providing access to a vast ecosystem of open-source libraries and modules. Developers can easily install, manage, and share packages to extend the functionality of their Node.js applications.

```
# Installing a package using npm
npm install package-name
```

**4. Full-Stack JavaScript Development:**

With Node.js on the server-side and JavaScript in the browser, developers can adopt a full-stack JavaScript approach, using a single language for both client and server applications. This unification simplifies development and reduces the need for context switching.

**5. Real-Time Applications:**

Node.js excels in building real-time applications like chat applications, online gaming platforms, and collaborative tools. Its event-driven nature and low-latency performance make it suitable for handling multiple simultaneous connections.

**6. RESTful APIs and Microservices:**

Node.js is commonly used to develop RESTful APIs and microservices due to its lightweight and fast nature. Developers can create scalable and responsive APIs for web and mobile applications.

```
// Creating a simple RESTful API with Express.js (a Node.js framework)
const express = require('express');
const app = express();
const port = 3000;

app.get('/api/users', (req, res) => {
  res.json({ users: ['Alice', 'Bob', 'Charlie'] });
});

app.listen(port, () => {
  console.log(`Server is listening at http://localhost:${port}`);
});
```

### 7. Scalability and Performance:

Node.js's ability to handle high levels of concurrency and its non-blocking architecture make it suitable for building scalable and performant applications. It is widely used by tech giants like Netflix, LinkedIn, and PayPal for their back-end services.

### 8. Serverless Computing:

Node.js plays a significant role in serverless computing platforms like AWS Lambda and Azure Functions. Developers can write serverless functions in JavaScript, enabling automatic scaling and cost optimization.

Node.js has revolutionized server-side development by introducing JavaScript as a powerful player in this domain. Its event-driven, non-blocking architecture, along with the npm ecosystem, has made it a favorite choice for building real-time applications, RESTful APIs, and scalable microservices. With Node.js, JavaScript's versatility extends beyond the browser, shaping the future of web development.

# Chapter 6: Python: The Language of Simplicity and Elegance

## 6.1 Python's Philosophy and Design Principles

Python is renowned for its simplicity and readability, which are at the core of its design philosophy. Guido van Rossum, the creator of Python, summarized this philosophy in the "Zen of Python" (PEP 20), a collection of aphorisms that capture the essence of Python's design principles. Let's explore some of these principles and how they influence Python's development:

- **Readability Counts**: Python code is meant to be easily readable and understandable. The use of indentation instead of braces for code blocks enforces a consistent and visually appealing structure.

- **Explicit is Better than Implicit**: Python encourages developers to write code that is explicit and clear. This promotes code that is less prone to ambiguity and surprises.

- **Simple is Better than Complex**: Python favors simplicity over complexity. When solving problems, Python developers strive to use straightforward and intuitive approaches.

- **Complex is Better than Complicated**: While simplicity is preferred, Python acknowledges that some problems are inherently complex. In such cases, Python aims to provide clear and elegant solutions.

- **Flat is Better than Nested**: Python discourages excessive nesting of code blocks. This helps maintain code clarity and prevents "deep" nesting that can make code hard to follow.

- **Sparse is Better than Dense**: Python code tends to be more spaced out and less dense, enhancing readability. This aligns with the idea that code is read more often than it is written.

- **Special Cases Aren't Special Enough to Break the Rules**: Python promotes consistency in coding conventions. Even though there might be exceptions, adhering to established rules is usually preferred.

- **Errors Should Never Pass Silently**: Python encourages error handling and reporting. When something goes wrong, Python raises exceptions to make issues explicit rather than letting them go unnoticed.

- **In the Face of Ambiguity, Refuse the Temptation to Guess**: Python emphasizes the importance of avoiding ambiguity in code. Instead of making assumptions, Python encourages explicit specifications.

- **There Should Be One—and Preferably Only One—Obvious Way to Do It**: Python promotes a single, clear way to perform tasks. This reduces confusion and debates over the "best" way to do something.

- **Now is Better than Never**: Python encourages taking action and making progress rather than waiting for the "perfect" solution. This pragmatic approach is valuable in software development.

Python's design principles have contributed to its widespread adoption and success in various domains, from web development to scientific computing. These principles make Python an ideal choice for both beginners and experienced developers, as it fosters a productive and enjoyable coding experience. In the following sections of this chapter, we will delve deeper into Python's features, its dynamic typing system, libraries, and its applications in data science, AI, scripting, automation, and web development.

## 6.2 Python's Interpreter and Dynamic Typing

Python's interpreter lies at the heart of the language's appeal. It enables developers to write and execute code interactively, making it easy to experiment and learn. In this section, we'll explore Python's interpreter and its key features.

### Interactive Mode

Python offers an interactive mode where you can type commands directly into the interpreter, and it immediately executes them. This interactive shell is an excellent tool for testing code snippets, debugging, and learning the language. You can launch the interactive interpreter by running python in your terminal.

```
$ python
Python 3.9.7 (default, Sep  3 2021, 14:55:47)
[GCC 8.4.0] on linux
Type "help", "copyright", "credits" or "license" for more information.
>>> print("Hello, Python!")
Hello, Python!
```

### Script Execution

Python also supports script execution. You can write Python code in a text file with a .py extension and execute it from the command line using the python command followed by the script's filename.

```
# hello.py
print("Hello, Python!")

$ python hello.py
Hello, Python!
```

### Dynamic Typing

Python is dynamically typed, which means that variable types are determined at runtime rather than being explicitly declared. This feature simplifies coding and makes Python more flexible. Here's an example:

```python
x = 5   # x is an integer
x = "Hello"   # x is now a string
x = [1, 2, 3]   # x is now a list
```

In this code, the variable x changes its type as different values are assigned to it. This dynamic typing allows for more versatile and concise code. However, it also requires careful attention to variable types to avoid unexpected behavior.

### Strong Typing

While Python is dynamically typed, it is also strongly typed. This means that Python enforces strict type checking and does not allow operations between incompatible types without explicit conversion. For example, you cannot add a string and an integer without converting one of them to the appropriate type:

```python
# This will raise a TypeError
result = "Hello, " + 5
```

To fix this, you need to convert the integer to a string:

```python
result = "Hello, " + str(5)
```

Python's combination of dynamic and strong typing helps prevent subtle bugs and promotes code reliability.

### Summary

Python's interactive mode, script execution, dynamic typing, and strong typing are essential features that contribute to its ease of use, versatility, and reliability. These characteristics make Python an excellent choice for a wide range of applications, from quick scripting tasks to complex software development and data analysis.

---

## 6.3 Libraries and Frameworks in Python

Python's extensive ecosystem of libraries and frameworks is one of its standout features. These libraries and frameworks provide pre-built solutions to various tasks, saving developers time and effort. In this section, we'll explore some of the essential libraries and frameworks in Python.

## Standard Library

Python's standard library is a collection of modules and packages that come bundled with Python itself. It covers a wide range of functionalities, from working with files and data to network communication and web development. Some notable modules include os for operating system interactions, datetime for working with dates and times, and json for handling JSON data.

```python
import os

# List all files in the current directory
files = os.listdir()
```

```python
import datetime

# Get the current date and time
now = datetime.datetime.now()
```

```python
import json

# Parse a JSON string
data = json.loads('{"name": "John", "age": 30}')
```

## NumPy

NumPy is a fundamental library for numerical and scientific computing in Python. It provides support for multidimensional arrays and matrices, along with a collection of mathematical functions to operate on these arrays. NumPy is widely used in fields like data analysis, machine learning, and scientific research.

```python
import numpy as np

# Create a NumPy array
arr = np.array([1, 2, 3, 4, 5])

# Perform mathematical operations on the array
mean = np.mean(arr)
```

## Pandas

Pandas is a library built on top of NumPy and provides powerful data structures and data analysis tools. It is particularly well-suited for handling structured data in tabular form, such as CSV files and SQL database tables. Pandas introduces the DataFrame, a versatile data structure for working with data.

```python
import pandas as pd

# Create a DataFrame from a CSV file
df = pd.read_csv('data.csv')
```

```python
# Perform operations on the DataFrame
mean_age = df['age'].mean()
```

Matplotlib

Matplotlib is a popular library for creating static, animated, and interactive visualizations in Python. It provides a wide range of plotting functions and customization options to create informative and visually appealing graphs and charts.

```python
import matplotlib.pyplot as plt

# Create a simple line plot
x = [1, 2, 3, 4, 5]
y = [10, 8, 6, 4, 2]
plt.plot(x, y)
plt.xlabel('X-axis')
plt.ylabel('Y-axis')
plt.title('Simple Line Plot')
plt.show()
```

Flask

Flask is a lightweight and flexible web framework for building web applications in Python. It is known for its simplicity and minimalism, making it an excellent choice for small to medium-sized web projects. Flask provides tools for routing, template rendering, and handling HTTP requests.

```python
from flask import Flask, render_template

app = Flask(__name__)

@app.route('/')
def hello_world():
    return 'Hello, Flask!'

if __name__ == '__main__':
    app.run()
```

Django

Django is a high-level web framework that follows the "batteries-included" philosophy, offering a comprehensive set of tools for building web applications. It provides features like authentication, database ORM, and a powerful admin interface, making it suitable for large and complex web projects.

```python
from django.shortcuts import render

def hello(request):
    return render(request, 'hello.html', {'message': 'Hello, Django!'})
```

These are just a few examples of the vast Python ecosystem. Whether you're working on data analysis, web development, machine learning, or scientific computing, Python's libraries and frameworks provide the tools you need to streamline your development process and build powerful applications efficiently.

---

## 6.4 Python in Data Science and AI

Python has gained immense popularity in the fields of data science and artificial intelligence (AI) due to its versatility, extensive libraries, and ease of use. In this section, we'll explore how Python is used in data science and AI applications.

### Data Science with Python

Python is the go-to language for data scientists and analysts. Its libraries and tools simplify tasks like data cleaning, exploration, and analysis. Some of the key libraries for data science in Python include:

1. *NumPy*: As mentioned earlier, NumPy is essential for numerical operations and working with arrays and matrices, making it a foundational tool for data manipulation.

2. *Pandas*: Pandas provides data structures like DataFrames and Series, making it easy to handle structured data. It offers functions for data indexing, merging, filtering, and aggregation.

3. *Matplotlib* and *Seaborn*: These libraries are used for data visualization. They allow data scientists to create various types of plots and charts to better understand data patterns.

4. *Scikit-Learn*: Scikit-Learn is a machine learning library that provides a wide range of algorithms for tasks like classification, regression, clustering, and dimensionality reduction.

5. *TensorFlow* and *PyTorch*: These deep learning frameworks are used for building and training neural networks. They are essential for AI applications, including image recognition, natural language processing, and reinforcement learning.

### AI and Machine Learning

Python's popularity in AI and machine learning is driven by its user-friendly libraries and frameworks. Here are some notable AI and machine learning libraries and tools in Python:

1. **Scikit-Learn**: *As mentioned earlier, Scikit-Learn is a versatile library for traditional machine learning tasks. It provides tools for data preprocessing, model selection, and evaluation.*

2. **TensorFlow** *and* **PyTorch**: *These deep learning frameworks are at the forefront of AI research and development. They offer high-level APIs for building complex neural networks and lower-level control for researchers and engineers.*

3. **Keras**: *Keras is a user-friendly, high-level neural networks API that runs on top of TensorFlow or other backends. It simplifies the process of building and training neural networks.*

4. **Natural Language Toolkit (NLTK)**: *NLTK is a library for natural language processing (NLP). It provides tools for tasks like tokenization, stemming, tagging, and parsing.*

5. **OpenCV**: *OpenCV is a computer vision library used for tasks like image and video processing, object detection, and facial recognition.*

### Jupyter Notebooks

Jupyter Notebooks are a popular choice for data scientists and researchers working in Python. They provide an interactive environment for combining code, visualizations, and explanatory text in a single document. Jupyter Notebooks are widely used for sharing and presenting data analysis and machine learning projects.

```python
# Example Jupyter Notebook cell
import pandas as pd

# Load a dataset
df = pd.read_csv('data.csv')

# Perform data analysis and visualization
```

### Conclusion

Python's versatility, rich ecosystem of libraries, and active community make it an ideal choice for data science and AI. Whether you're analyzing data, building machine learning models, or working on advanced AI projects, Python provides the tools and support you need to succeed in these rapidly growing fields.

---

## 6.5 Scripting, Automation, and Web Development with Python

Python's versatility extends beyond data science and AI; it's also a powerful language for scripting, automation, and web development. In this section, we'll explore how Python is used in these domains.

## Scripting

Python's simplicity and readability make it an excellent choice for scripting tasks. Whether you need to automate repetitive tasks, process files, or manipulate data, Python provides the tools to get the job done efficiently.

Here's a simple example of a Python script that renames multiple files in a directory:

```python
import os

# List all files in the directory
files = os.listdir()

# Rename files with a specific prefix
prefix = "new_"
for file in files:
    if file.endswith(".txt"):
        new_name = prefix + file
        os.rename(file, new_name)
```

## Automation

Python excels in automation, allowing you to streamline workflows and reduce manual intervention. It can automate tasks like sending emails, managing files, and interacting with external systems.

For instance, you can use Python's smtplib library to send emails programmatically:

```python
import smtplib
from email.mime.text import MIMEText
from email.mime.multipart import MIMEMultipart

# Email configuration
sender_email = "your_email@gmail.com"
receiver_email = "recipient_email@gmail.com"
password = "your_password"

# Create the email content
message = MIMEMultipart()
message["From"] = sender_email
message["To"] = receiver_email
message["Subject"] = "Automated Email"

body = "This is an automated email sent from Python."
message.attach(MIMEText(body, "plain"))

# Send the email
try:
    server = smtplib.SMTP("smtp.gmail.com", 587)
    server.starttls()
```

```
    server.login(sender_email, password)
    text = message.as_string()
    server.sendmail(sender_email, receiver_email, text)
    server.quit()
    print("Email sent successfully!")
except Exception as e:
    print(f"Email could not be sent. Error: {e}")
```

Web Development

Python offers several web frameworks for building web applications. Two popular choices are Flask and Django, each catering to different needs.

*Flask*

Flask is a lightweight web framework that's easy to get started with. It's suitable for small to medium-sized web projects and follows a minimalist philosophy. Flask provides the essentials for routing, request handling, and template rendering while allowing you to add additional libraries as needed.

```
from flask import Flask, render_template

app = Flask(__name__)

@app.route('/')
def home():
    return render_template('index.html')

if __name__ == '__main__':
    app.run()
```

*Django*

Django, on the other hand, is a full-fledged web framework that includes features like an ORM, authentication, and an admin interface. It's well-suited for larger, more complex web applications.

```
from django.shortcuts import render

def home(request):
    return render(request, 'home.html')
```

Both Flask and Django have vibrant communities and extensive documentation, making web development in Python accessible to developers at all levels.

Conclusion

Python's versatility as a scripting language, automation tool, and web development platform has made it a favorite among developers across various domains. Whether you're writing scripts to simplify daily tasks, automating complex workflows, or building web applications, Python's simplicity and extensive libraries make it a reliable choice.

## 7.1 Understanding Syntax in Programming Languages

In the world of programming languages, syntax refers to the set of rules that dictate how programs written in that language must be structured. Syntax serves as the foundation upon which code is written, and understanding it is essential for any developer. In this section, we will explore the significance of syntax in programming languages and how it influences the way code is written and interpreted.

### Importance of Syntax

Syntax plays a crucial role in programming languages for several reasons:

1. **Code Readability:** Clear and consistent syntax makes code easier to read and understand. Developers often spend more time reading code than writing it, so well-structured code with a consistent syntax is essential for collaboration and maintainability.

2. **Error Detection:** Syntax rules help identify and prevent errors. When code follows the correct syntax, it is more likely to be error-free, reducing the need for debugging.

3. **Interpretation and Compilation:** The interpreter or compiler of a programming language relies on syntax to understand and process code. Correct syntax ensures that programs can be executed or compiled successfully.

4. **Standardization:** Syntax provides a standardized way of expressing instructions and data. This standardization allows different developers to work on the same codebase and ensures portability across different platforms.

### Syntax Elements

Programming languages consist of various syntax elements, including:

### 1. Keywords

Keywords are reserved words in a programming language that have predefined meanings. They cannot be used as identifiers (e.g., variable or function names) and are an integral part of the language's syntax. Examples include "if," "else," "while," and "for" in many languages.

### 2. Operators

Operators are symbols or keywords used to perform operations on data. They define how data is manipulated in expressions. Common operators include "+," "-", "*","/", and"==".

### 3. Variables

Variables are used to store and manipulate data. They have names (identifiers) and data types associated with them, and their declaration and usage must adhere to the language's syntax rules.

### 4. Statements

Statements are individual instructions that make up a program. They typically end with a semicolon in languages like C, C++, and Java. Statements must follow the language's syntax for proper execution.

### 5. Brackets and Delimiters

Brackets, such as curly braces "{ }" and parentheses "( )", are used to define the scope and grouping of code blocks. Delimiters, like commas "," and colons ":", are used to separate elements or indicate the beginning of blocks.

## Language-Specific Syntax

Each programming language has its own unique syntax rules. For example, C and C++ use curly braces to define code blocks, while Python uses indentation. Understanding the syntax of a particular language is essential for writing correct code in that language.

```c
// Example C code with curly braces
#include <stdio.h>

int main() {
    int x = 10;
    if (x > 5) {
        printf("x is greater than 5\n");
    }
    return 0;
}
```

```python
# Example Python code with indentation
x = 10
if x > 5:
    print("x is greater than 5")
```

## Syntax Errors

When code violates the syntax rules of a programming language, it results in syntax errors. These errors must be corrected before the code can be executed or compiled. Syntax errors are often detected by the language's interpreter or compiler and reported to the developer.

## Conclusion

Syntax is the backbone of programming languages, defining how code is structured and understood by both developers and computers. A solid grasp of syntax is fundamental for writing readable, error-free, and functional code. As you explore different programming languages, pay close attention to their unique syntax rules to become an effective and proficient developer in each language.

---

## 7.2 The Role of Semantics in Code Execution

While syntax governs the structure and form of a program, semantics define its meaning and behavior. In this section, we'll delve into the significance of semantics in programming languages and how they influence code execution.

### Understanding Semantics

Semantics deals with the interpretation and execution of code. It defines how the code should behave, what operations it should perform, and how data should be manipulated. While syntax ensures that code is well-formed and adheres to the language's rules, semantics ensure that code behaves as intended.

### Key Aspects of Semantics

1. **Variable Assignments:** Semantics dictate how variables are assigned values, how they store data, and how operations are performed on them. For example, in Python, variables are dynamically typed, meaning their data type can change during execution.

2. **Control Flow:** Semantics define the order in which statements are executed, how conditional statements determine branching, and how loops control repetition. Control flow semantics ensure that code executes logically and produces the desired output.

3. **Function Calls:** The semantics of function calls specify how arguments are passed to functions, how return values are handled, and how function scope affects variable visibility.

4. **Data Manipulation:** Semantics govern how data is manipulated using operators, expressions, and built-in functions. Different languages may have different semantics for data manipulation, even with similar syntax.

### Language-Specific Semantics

Every programming language has its own set of semantics, and these can vary significantly from one language to another. For instance, in JavaScript, asynchronous operations and callback functions are fundamental to its semantics, enabling non-blocking code execution. In contrast, C++ emphasizes manual memory management as a core semantic feature.

### Handling Semantic Errors

Unlike syntax errors, which are typically detected by the interpreter or compiler, semantic errors are often more subtle and harder to detect. These errors result from incorrect logic or the misuse of language features, leading to unexpected behavior.

Here's an example of a semantic error in Python:

```
# Semantic error: Incorrect calculation
x = 5
y = "2"
result = x + y  # Attempting to add an integer and a string
print(result)
```

In this code, the semantic error arises from trying to add an integer and a string, which is not a valid operation in Python. The program will run, but the result will not be as expected.

### Importance of Semantics

Understanding the semantics of a programming language is crucial for writing correct and efficient code. It allows developers to express their intentions accurately and ensures that the code behaves as desired. Additionally, knowing the semantics of a language enables developers to troubleshoot and debug code effectively, as they can identify and rectify semantic errors.

In conclusion, while syntax defines how code should look, semantics define how it should behave. Both aspects are essential for effective programming, and a thorough understanding of semantics is vital for writing code that not only compiles but also functions correctly.

## 7.3 Comparing Syntax Across Different Languages

Programming languages vary significantly in terms of syntax, making it crucial for developers to adapt to different language constructs when working on diverse projects. In this section, we will explore the differences and similarities in syntax among programming languages and discuss the challenges and benefits of this diversity.

### Syntax Diversity

Programming languages have evolved over time to cater to different domains and paradigms, resulting in a wide range of syntax structures. Some languages emphasize concise and expressive syntax, while others prioritize explicitness and control. For example, Python is known for its clean and readable syntax, while languages like C and C++ offer low-level control and flexibility.

Here's a brief comparison of syntax elements across different languages:

- **Variable Declaration:** In C and C++, variables are declared with explicit data types (e.g., `int x;`). In Python, data types are dynamically inferred (e.g., `x = 5`).

- **Looping Constructs:** The syntax for loops varies; C uses `for` loops with explicit control, Python uses `for` loops that iterate over iterable objects, and JavaScript provides both `for` and `forEach` constructs.

- **Function Definitions:** In C++, functions are explicitly defined with a return type (e.g., `int add(int a, int b) { return a + b; }`), while Python defines functions without explicit types (e.g., `def add(a, b): return a + b`).

- **Conditional Statements:** Syntax for conditionals also varies; C uses `if`, `else if`, and `else`, Python uses `if`, `elif`, and `else`, and JavaScript uses `if`, `else if`, and `else`.

## Benefits of Syntax Diversity

1. **Domain-Specific Languages (DSLs):** Some languages are designed for specific domains, such as SQL for databases or HTML/CSS for web development. These languages have syntax tailored to their respective purposes, making them more efficient for specific tasks.

2. **Expressiveness:** Diverse syntax allows developers to choose languages that match their problem-solving style. Some may prefer the conciseness of Python, while others may prefer the control offered by C++.

3. **Language Interoperability:** In software development, it's common to use multiple languages within a project. Diverse syntax enables developers to select the best language for each task while maintaining compatibility.

## Challenges of Syntax Diversity

1. **Learning Curve:** Learning and mastering multiple languages with different syntax can be challenging for developers, especially beginners.

2. **Maintenance:** Projects that use multiple languages with varying syntax can be complex to maintain, requiring expertise in each language.

3. **Integration:** Integrating code written in different languages can be challenging due to differences in syntax, data structures, and calling conventions.

4. **Error-Prone:** Switching between languages with different syntax can lead to syntax errors when developers make mistakes related to the syntax of the current language they are working in.

## Cross-Language Development

Modern software development often involves working with multiple languages. For example, a web developer might use JavaScript for frontend development, Python for backend server logic, and SQL for database queries. To navigate the complexities of syntax diversity, developers rely on tools, libraries, and frameworks that provide seamless integration between languages and simplify the development process.

In conclusion, the diversity of syntax in programming languages reflects the versatility of languages and their suitability for various tasks. While it presents challenges, such as a steep learning curve and increased complexity, it also offers benefits in terms of expressiveness and domain-specific optimization. As developers, understanding and adapting to different syntax structures is an essential skill in a rapidly evolving technology landscape.

## 7.4 Error Handling and Debugging

Error handling and debugging are integral parts of software development. In this section, we'll explore how different programming languages approach error handling and debugging, and we'll discuss the tools and techniques commonly used to identify and resolve issues in code.

### Error Handling

*C and C++*

In C and C++, error handling is often accomplished through return values and error codes. Functions that can encounter errors return specific error codes or use sentinel values (e.g., -1) to indicate failure. Developers are responsible for checking these return values and taking appropriate actions when errors occur.

```
FILE* file = fopen("example.txt", "r");
if (file == NULL) {
    perror("Error opening file");
    // Handle the error
} else {
    // Continue with file operations
}
```

*Python*

Python adopts a different approach to error handling using exceptions. When an error occurs, Python raises an exception, and the program's flow is disrupted until the exception is caught and handled by an exception handler. Python encourages the use of try, except, and finally blocks for robust error handling.

```
try:
    result = 10 / 0
except ZeroDivisionError as e:
    print("Error:", e)
    # Handle the error gracefully
```

86

## Debugging

*C and C++*

Debugging in C and C++ often involves the use of debuggers like GDB. Developers can set breakpoints, examine variable values, and step through code to identify and fix issues. Printing debugging information using `printf` statements is also a common practice.

```c
int main() {
    int x = 10;
    printf("Value of x: %d\n", x);
    // Insert breakpoints and debug the program
    return 0;
}
```

*Python*

Python offers a range of debugging tools, including the built-in `pdb` debugger. Developers can insert breakpoints, inspect variables, and step through code interactively. Integrated development environments (IDEs) like PyCharm provide graphical debugging interfaces.

```python
import pdb

def divide(x, y):
    result = x / y
    return result

pdb.set_trace()   # Start debugging here
result = divide(10, 0)
```

### Challenges and Best Practices

1. **Language-Specific Debugging:** Each language has its debugging tools and conventions. Developers working with multiple languages must become proficient in each language's debugging techniques.

2. **Error Propagation:** In languages like C++, proper error propagation through return values or exceptions is crucial to ensure errors are handled effectively.

3. **Logging:** Logging is essential for tracking the flow of code execution and recording errors. Logging frameworks like `log4j` (Java) or `logging` (Python) can be beneficial.

4. **Unit Testing:** Writing unit tests can help catch errors early in the development process and ensure that code functions correctly.

5. **Code Reviews:** Peer code reviews are an effective way to identify and rectify errors before they make it into the codebase.

6. **Static Analysis Tools:** Tools like linters and static analyzers can detect potential issues in code before it is executed.

In conclusion, error handling and debugging are essential skills for developers. Different programming languages provide unique approaches and tools for these tasks. Understanding the error handling and debugging mechanisms of the language you are working with is crucial for writing robust and error-free code.

## 7.5 Best Practices for Readable and Maintainable Code

Writing code that is not only functional but also readable and maintainable is a critical aspect of software development. Code is often read and modified by multiple developers throughout its lifecycle, making it essential to follow best practices that enhance clarity and ease of maintenance.

### 1. Meaningful Variable and Function Names

Choose descriptive and meaningful names for variables and functions. Names should indicate the purpose or role of the entity they represent. Avoid single-letter or cryptic names that can confuse readers.

**Bad:**

```
s = "Hello, World"
```

**Good:**

```
greeting_message = "Hello, World"
```

### 2. Consistent Indentation and Formatting

Adhere to consistent indentation and formatting standards. Use spaces or tabs consistently for indentation and follow a consistent coding style throughout the project. Tools like linters can help enforce code formatting.

**Bad:**

```
if condition:
result = perform_action()
```

**Good:**

```
if condition:
    result = perform_action()
```

### 3. Comments and Documentation

Document your code using meaningful comments and docstrings. Explain the purpose of functions, classes, and complex logic. Well-documented code is easier for others (and your future self) to understand.

```python
def calculate_average(numbers):
    """
    Calculate the average of a list of numbers.

    Args:
        numbers (list): List of numbers to calculate the average for.

    Returns:
        float: The average value.
    """
    total = sum(numbers)
    return total / len(numbers)
```

## 4. Modularization

Break down code into modular and reusable components. Use functions or classes to encapsulate specific functionality. This promotes code reusability and simplifies testing.

**Bad:**

```python
# Single monolithic function
def process_data(data):
    # Complex and lengthy logic here
```

**Good:**

```python
# Modular approach
def validate_data(data):
    # Validation logic

def transform_data(data):
    # Transformation logic

def load_data(data):
    # Loading logic
```

## 5. Avoid Magic Numbers and Hardcoding

Avoid using magic numbers (unexplained constants) and hardcoding values throughout your code. Instead, use named constants or configuration settings that make it easier to update values in one place.

**Bad:**

```python
if status_code == 404:
    # Handle not found
```

**Good:**

```python
NOT_FOUND_STATUS_CODE = 404
```

```
if status_code == NOT_FOUND_STATUS_CODE:
    # Handle not found
```

## 6. Version Control and Collaboration

Use version control systems like Git to track changes and collaborate effectively with team members. Create branches for feature development and use pull requests for code review.

## 7. Unit Testing

Implement unit tests for your code to ensure that it functions correctly and reliably. Unit tests catch regressions and help maintain code integrity when making changes.

## 8. Refactoring

Periodically review and refactor code to improve its structure and maintainability. Refactoring is an essential part of keeping codebases clean and efficient.

## 9. Follow Language Best Practices

Each programming language has its best practices and idioms. Familiarize yourself with these language-specific guidelines to write code that aligns with community standards.

In summary, writing readable and maintainable code is crucial for the long-term success of a software project. By following these best practices, you can make your code more understandable, less error-prone, and easier for others to work with and extend.

# Chapter 8: Data Types and Structures

## 8.1 Primitive Data Types Across Languages

Data types are a fundamental concept in programming languages. They define the kind of data a variable can hold and the operations that can be performed on it. While different programming languages may have their own data types, there are common primitive data types that exist across many languages. In this section, we'll explore these primitive data types and how they are represented in various languages.

### Integer Types

Integers represent whole numbers, both positive and negative. Most programming languages offer various sizes of integer types, such as:

- **int**: A standard integer type.
- **long** or **int64**: A larger integer type capable of holding larger values.
- **short** or **int16**: A smaller integer type with a limited range.

Here's how integers are represented in different languages:

*C and C++*

In C and C++, you can use keywords like int, long, and short to declare integer types:

```
int myInteger = 42;
long myLongInteger = 1234567890;
short myShortInteger = 10;
```

*Java*

Java provides integer types with specified sizes:

```
int myInteger = 42;
long myLongInteger = 1234567890L; // Note the 'L' suffix for long
short myShortInteger = 10;
```

*Python*

Python's integer type can automatically adjust in size as needed:

```
my_integer = 42
my_long_integer = 12345678901234567890
```

### Floating-Point Types

Floating-point types are used to represent real numbers with decimal points. These types include:

- **float**: Single-precision floating-point.

- **double**: Double-precision floating-point, which provides greater precision.
- **decimal**: A decimal floating-point type with fixed precision for financial calculations (not available in all languages).

Here's how floating-point numbers are represented in different languages:

*C and C++*

In C and C++, you can use float and double to declare floating-point types:

```
float myFloat = 3.14;
double myDouble = 3.141592653589793;
```

*Java*

Java provides float and double for floating-point numbers:

```
float myFloat = 3.14F; // Note the 'F' suffix for float
double myDouble = 3.141592653589793;
```

*Python*

Python uses a single float type for floating-point numbers:

```
my_float = 3.14
```

## Boolean Type

The boolean type represents true or false values. In most programming languages, this type is called bool or boolean:

*C and C++*

C and C++ use the _Bool type, which can be used as bool through macros:

```
_Bool myBool = 1; // 1 represents true
```

*Java*

Java uses the boolean type:

```
boolean myBoolean = true;
```

*Python*

Python uses bool:

```
my_bool = True
```

## Character Types

Character types are used to represent individual characters, such as letters, digits, or symbols. In C and C++, char is used for this purpose:

*C and C++*
```
char myChar = 'A';
```

In Java, the char type is used similarly:

*Java*
```
char myChar = 'A';
```

Python, on the other hand, doesn't have a separate character type. Instead, you can use a string of length 1 to represent a character:

*Python*
```
my_char = 'A'
```

### Conclusion

These are some of the common primitive data types that exist across programming languages. Understanding data types is essential for writing code that is both correct and efficient. While the specific names and sizes of these types may vary between languages, the fundamental concepts remain consistent. In the next sections, we'll explore more complex data structures and their implementations in different languages.

---

## 8.2 Complex Data Structures and Their Implementation

In addition to primitive data types, programming languages provide complex data structures to efficiently organize and manipulate larger amounts of data. These structures offer various ways to store, retrieve, and process information, making them essential tools for software development. Let's explore some common complex data structures and their implementation in different programming languages.

### Arrays

Arrays are one of the simplest complex data structures, allowing you to store a collection of elements of the same data type in a contiguous memory block. They are indexed by integers and provide constant-time access to elements. Here's how you can use arrays in different languages:

*C and C++*

In C and C++, you can declare arrays like this:

```
int myArray[5] = {1, 2, 3, 4, 5};
```

Accessing elements:

```
int element = myArray[2]; // Retrieves the third element (index 2)
```

In Java, arrays are declared as follows:

```
int[] myArray = {1, 2, 3, 4, 5};
```

Accessing elements:

```
int element = myArray[2]; // Retrieves the third element (index 2)
```

*Python*

Python has built-in lists that can be used like arrays:

```
my_list = [1, 2, 3, 4, 5]
```

Accessing elements:

```
element = my_list[2]   # Retrieves the third element (index 2)
```

## Lists (Dynamic Arrays)

Lists, also known as dynamic arrays, are resizable arrays that automatically adjust their size as elements are added or removed. They are available in languages like Python and Java:

*Java*

In Java, ArrayLists provide dynamic arrays:

```
import java.util.ArrayList;

ArrayList<Integer> myList = new ArrayList<>();
myList.add(1);
myList.add(2);
myList.add(3);
```

*Python*

Python's lists are dynamic arrays by default:

```
my_list = [1, 2, 3]
my_list.append(4)
my_list.remove(2)
```

## Linked Lists

Linked lists are data structures consisting of nodes, where each node contains a value and a reference (or link) to the next node in the sequence. They can be singly linked (each node points to the next) or doubly linked (each node points to both the next and the previous nodes). Linked lists are often used when frequent insertions and deletions are required. Here's how you can implement linked lists in C++, Java, and Python:

In C++, you can define a linked list using custom classes:

```cpp
struct Node {
    int data;
    Node* next;
};

Node* head = nullptr; // Initialize an empty linked list
```

*Java*

In Java, you can define a singly linked list:

```java
class Node {
    int data;
    Node next;

    Node(int data) {
        this.data = data;
        this.next = null;
    }
}

Node head = null; // Initialize an empty linked list
```

*Python*

In Python, you can implement a singly linked list using classes:

```python
class Node:
    def __init__(self, data):
        self.data = data
        self.next = None

head = None  # Initialize an empty linked list
```

## Conclusion

Complex data structures, such as arrays, lists, and linked lists, are essential components of programming languages. They provide flexibility and efficiency in managing data, allowing developers to create more sophisticated and optimized algorithms. Understanding these structures and how to implement them in different languages is crucial for effective software development. In the next section, we'll explore memory allocation for data types and discuss how it differs across various programming languages.

## 8.3 Memory Allocation for Data Types

Memory allocation is a fundamental concept in programming languages, as it determines how and where data is stored in a computer's memory. Different data types require varying amounts of memory, and languages handle memory allocation differently. Let's delve into memory allocation for data types and explore the strategies employed by various programming languages.

### Stack and Heap Allocation

Most programming languages allocate memory in two primary areas: the stack and the heap.

#### Stack Allocation

- **Stack**: The stack is a region of memory that is used for storing local variables and function call information. It follows a Last-In, First-Out (LIFO) order, where the most recently allocated memory is the first to be deallocated.
- **Data Types**: Primitive data types, such as integers, floating-point numbers, and pointers, are typically stored on the stack. These data types have fixed sizes, making stack allocation efficient.

#### Heap Allocation

- **Heap**: The heap is a region of memory used for dynamic memory allocation. Data allocated on the heap persists beyond the scope of a function and requires manual deallocation.
- **Data Types**: Complex data structures like arrays, strings, and objects with variable sizes are often allocated on the heap. Languages like C and C++ provide functions like `malloc` and `free` to manage heap memory.

### Automatic vs. Manual Memory Management

Languages handle memory management in two primary ways: automatic and manual.

#### Automatic Memory Management

- **Automatic**: Languages like Python, Java, and JavaScript use automatic memory management through mechanisms like garbage collection. These languages automatically track and reclaim memory that is no longer in use, reducing the risk of memory leaks.
- **Advantages**: Simplifies memory management for developers, reduces the risk of memory-related bugs, and enhances code safety.

#### Manual Memory Management

- **Manual**: Languages like C and C++ offer manual memory management, requiring developers to explicitly allocate and deallocate memory. This gives programmers fine-grained control over memory but increases the risk of memory leaks and bugs if not managed properly.

- **Advantages**: Allows precise control over memory allocation and deallocation, enabling efficient resource utilization.

Garbage Collection Mechanisms

Languages with automatic memory management employ various garbage collection mechanisms to identify and reclaim unused memory.

*Java*

- Java uses a generational garbage collector, categorizing objects into young and old generations. Young objects are collected more frequently, while older objects are collected less often to optimize performance.

*Python*

- Python employs reference counting and cyclic garbage collection. It keeps track of reference counts for objects and periodically identifies and collects cyclic references.

Conclusion

Memory allocation is a crucial aspect of programming languages, influencing both the efficiency and safety of code. Understanding how data types are allocated, whether on the stack or heap, and the memory management mechanisms in place is essential for writing robust and efficient programs. In the next section, we'll explore memory optimization strategies, including techniques to prevent memory leaks and improve resource utilization.

---

## 8.4 Comparing Data Handling in C, C++, Java, JavaScript, and Python

Data handling is a fundamental aspect of programming, and different programming languages provide varying mechanisms for working with data. In this section, we'll compare how data is handled in C, C++, Java, JavaScript, and Python, highlighting the strengths and weaknesses of each language in terms of data manipulation and management.

C

C is a low-level programming language known for its simplicity and efficiency. Data handling in C involves manual memory management and explicit type declarations.

- **Data Types**: C offers a variety of primitive data types, including integers, floating-point numbers, characters, and pointers. Custom data structures are created using structs.
- **Memory Management**: Memory allocation and deallocation are manual tasks in C, using functions like `malloc` and `free`. This provides precise control but requires careful management to prevent memory leaks and segmentation faults.

- **Type System**: C has a weak type system, allowing for flexible data manipulation but potentially leading to type-related errors if not handled carefully.
- **Arrays**: Arrays in C are fixed-size and can be multi-dimensional. However, they lack bounds checking, which can lead to buffer overflow vulnerabilities if not managed properly.

## C++

C++ is an extension of C with added features, including support for object-oriented programming. It provides more advanced data handling capabilities.

- **Data Types**: C++ inherits C's primitive data types but adds classes and objects for implementing user-defined data structures.
- **Memory Management**: C++ supports manual memory management using new and delete operators but also offers smart pointers for automatic memory management. This provides a balance between control and convenience.
- **Type System**: C++ has a stronger type system compared to C, reducing the risk of type-related errors.
- **STL**: The Standard Template Library (STL) in C++ provides a rich set of data structures and algorithms, simplifying data manipulation tasks.

## Java

Java is known for its portability and strong memory management. It uses automatic memory management through garbage collection.

- **Data Types**: Java provides a set of primitive data types (e.g., int, float) and objects for more complex data structures. All user-defined types are derived from classes.
- **Memory Management**: Java features automatic memory management, where the garbage collector automatically reclaims memory that is no longer in use. This reduces the risk of memory leaks but can introduce overhead.
- **Type System**: Java enforces a strong type system, enhancing type safety and reducing type-related errors.
- **Collections Framework**: Java includes a Collections Framework with a wide range of data structures like ArrayLists, HashMaps, and LinkedLists, simplifying data manipulation.

## JavaScript

JavaScript is a dynamically typed scripting language widely used for web development. It offers flexibility but requires careful handling.

- **Data Types**: JavaScript includes primitive data types like numbers, strings, and booleans, as well as complex types such as objects and arrays. Its dynamic typing allows variables to change types during runtime.

- **Memory Management**: JavaScript uses automatic memory management with a garbage collector, making it developer-friendly by eliminating manual memory management tasks.
- **Type System**: JavaScript's dynamic typing can lead to unexpected type-related issues if not carefully managed.
- **Objects and Prototypes**: JavaScript relies heavily on objects and prototypal inheritance, which can be powerful but may also introduce complexity.

Python

Python is known for its simplicity and readability, offering dynamic typing and automatic memory management.

- **Data Types**: Python includes a wide range of built-in data types, such as integers, floats, strings, lists, and dictionaries. Its dynamic typing allows for flexible data manipulation.
- **Memory Management**: Python employs automatic memory management through reference counting and garbage collection, reducing the risk of memory-related bugs.
- **Type System**: Python's dynamic typing allows for more flexible coding but may require careful handling to avoid unexpected type-related issues.
- **Libraries**: Python has a rich ecosystem of libraries and frameworks, making it easy to work with various data types and perform complex data manipulations.

In summary, each programming language has its own approach to data handling, with advantages and trade-offs. The choice of language depends on factors like the project's requirements, development team expertise, and desired level of control over memory management and data manipulation. Understanding these differences can help programmers make informed decisions when selecting a language for a particular task.

## 8.5 Efficient Data Manipulation Techniques

Efficient data manipulation is a crucial aspect of programming, as it directly impacts the performance and functionality of software applications. In this section, we will explore various techniques for optimizing data manipulation in programming languages like C, C++, Java, JavaScript, and Python.

C and C++

*Pointers and Memory Layout*

C and C++ provide direct access to memory through pointers. Efficient data manipulation often involves pointer arithmetic and working with memory layouts. By carefully managing memory and minimizing unnecessary copying, developers can achieve high performance in these languages. However, improper memory management can lead to memory leaks and bugs like buffer overflows.

### Low-Level Operations

C and C++ offer low-level operations for bitwise manipulation, which can be extremely efficient for specific tasks. For example, using bitwise operations to manipulate individual bits in integers or characters can lead to compact and fast code.

### Inline Assembly

In C and C++, developers can use inline assembly to write machine-specific code for optimized data manipulation. While this provides fine-grained control, it can be challenging and platform-dependent.

## Java

### Java Collections Framework

Java's Collections Framework provides efficient data structures like ArrayLists, HashMaps, and LinkedLists. Choosing the right data structure for a specific task can significantly impact performance. ArrayLists, for instance, are efficient for random access, while LinkedLists are suitable for frequent insertions and deletions.

### Stream API

Java's Stream API allows developers to express data manipulation operations in a functional and declarative style. It provides a concise and readable way to perform operations like filtering, mapping, and reducing on collections.

## JavaScript

### Array Methods

JavaScript provides built-in array methods like `map`, `filter`, `reduce`, and `forEach` that allow developers to manipulate arrays efficiently. These methods are highly optimized in modern JavaScript engines.

### Avoiding Synchronous Operations

In JavaScript, avoiding synchronous operations and utilizing asynchronous programming with callbacks or Promises can improve performance. This is crucial for handling I/O-bound tasks without blocking the event loop.

## Python

### List Comprehensions

Python's list comprehensions provide a concise and efficient way to create lists and perform operations on them. They are often faster than equivalent for loops.

Python offers built-in functions like map, filter, and reduce that can enhance code readability and performance when working with iterable data structures.

*NumPy*

For scientific and numeric computing, Python's NumPy library provides highly efficient data manipulation capabilities. NumPy arrays are designed for fast numerical operations and support vectorized operations, which can significantly speed up computations.

## General Tips

Regardless of the programming language, some general tips can help improve data manipulation efficiency:

- Minimize data copying: Avoid unnecessary copying of data, as it can be a performance bottleneck.
- Profile and optimize: Use profiling tools to identify performance bottlenecks in your code and focus optimization efforts on critical sections.
- Choose the right algorithm and data structure: Selecting the appropriate algorithm and data structure for a specific task can have a substantial impact on efficiency.
- Leverage parallelism and concurrency: In multi-core systems, parallel processing and concurrency can be used to speed up data manipulation tasks.

Efficient data manipulation is essential for writing high-performance software. Developers should be mindful of the programming language's features and best practices to achieve optimal performance while maintaining code readability and maintainability.

# Chapter 9: Control Structures and Flow

## 9.1 Understanding Conditional Statements

Conditional statements are fundamental control structures in programming that allow you to make decisions in your code based on specific conditions. These statements enable you to create branches in your program's execution, making it responsive and adaptable. In this section, we will explore conditional statements in various programming languages, including C, C++, Java, JavaScript, and Python.

### The If Statement

*C and C++*

In C and C++, the if statement is used for conditional branching. It evaluates a boolean expression and executes a block of code if the condition is true. Here's a basic example in C:

```c
if (condition) {
    // Code to execute when the condition is true
} else {
    // Code to execute when the condition is false
}
```

*Java*

Java follows a similar syntax for the if statement:

```java
if (condition) {
    // Code to execute when the condition is true
} else {
    // Code to execute when the condition is false
}
```

*JavaScript*

In JavaScript, the if statement is used for conditional execution:

```javascript
if (condition) {
    // Code to execute when the condition is true
} else {
    // Code to execute when the condition is false
}
```

*Python*

Python's if statement is concise and easy to read:

```python
if condition:
    # Code to execute when the condition is true
```

```
else:
    # Code to execute when the condition is false
```

## The Switch Statement

*C and C++*

C and C++ provide the switch statement for multi-way branching. It evaluates an expression and executes code blocks based on the value of the expression. Here's a C example:

```
switch (expression) {
    case value1:
        // Code to execute when expression matches value1
        break;
    case value2:
        // Code to execute when expression matches value2
        break;
    default:
        // Code to execute when no case matches
}
```

*Java*

Java also includes the switch statement:

```
switch (expression) {
    case value1:
        // Code to execute when expression matches value1
        break;
    case value2:
        // Code to execute when expression matches value2
        break;
    default:
        // Code to execute when no case matches
}
```

## The Ternary Operator

*All Languages*

The ternary operator is a concise way to write conditional expressions in all the mentioned languages. It has the following syntax:

```
result = value_if_true if condition else value_if_false
```

## Conditional Statements Best Practices
- Keep conditions simple and readable.
- Use indentation and formatting to make your code clear.
- Avoid nested conditional statements when possible for better code maintainability.
- Use the ternary operator for concise conditional expressions.

- Document your code to explain complex or unusual conditions.

Conditional statements are vital for creating dynamic and responsive programs. They allow you to control the flow of your code and make decisions based on specific conditions, enhancing the functionality of your software.

---

## 9.2 Loop Constructs Across Different Languages

Loop constructs are essential for performing repetitive tasks in programming. They allow you to execute a block of code multiple times, which is particularly useful when dealing with collections of data, iterating through elements, or implementing algorithms. In this section, we will explore loop constructs in several programming languages, including C, C++, Java, JavaScript, and Python.

### The For Loop

*C and C++*

In C and C++, the for loop is commonly used for iterating through a range of values. It has the following syntax:

```c
for (initialization; condition; increment/decrement) {
    // Code to execute in each iteration
}
```

Here's an example that prints numbers from 1 to 5 in C:

```c
for (int i = 1; i <= 5; i++) {
    printf("%d ", i);
}
```

*Java*

Java also uses the for loop with a similar syntax:

```java
for (initialization; condition; increment/decrement) {
    // Code to execute in each iteration
}
```

Here's the same example in Java:

```java
for (int i = 1; i <= 5; i++) {
    System.out.print(i + " ");
}
```

*JavaScript*

In JavaScript, the for loop is quite versatile. It can iterate through arrays, objects, or a range of values:

```
for (initialization; condition; increment/decrement) {
    // Code to execute in each iteration
}
```

Here's an example of iterating through an array in JavaScript:

```
const numbers = [1, 2, 3, 4, 5];
for (let i = 0; i < numbers.length; i++) {
    console.log(numbers[i]);
}
```

*Python*

Python uses the for-in loop, which is designed for iterating over collections like lists, tuples, and dictionaries:

```
for element in iterable:
    # Code to execute in each iteration
```

Here's an example of iterating through a list in Python:

```
numbers = [1, 2, 3, 4, 5]
for num in numbers:
    print(num)
```

The While Loop

*All Languages*

The while loop is used for indefinite iteration until a certain condition is met. It has the following syntax:

```
while (condition) {
    // Code to execute as long as the condition is true
}
```

Here's an example of a while loop in Python:

```
count = 1
while count <= 5:
    print(count)
    count += 1
```

## The Do-While Loop

C and C++ also support the do-while loop, which ensures that the loop body is executed at least once, even if the condition is false afterward. It has the following syntax:

```c
do {
    // Code to execute
} while (condition);
```

Here's an example in C:

```c
int count = 1;
do {
    printf("%d ", count);
    count++;
} while (count <= 5);
```

Loop constructs are fundamental in programming and allow you to automate repetitive tasks efficiently. Depending on the language, you can choose the loop construct that best suits your specific needs, whether it's iterating through data structures, performing calculations, or controlling program flow.

---

## 9.3 Recursive Functions and Their Usage

Recursion is a powerful programming concept that allows a function to call itself. Recursive functions are used when a problem can be divided into smaller, similar sub-problems. In this section, we will explore recursive functions and their usage in various programming languages, including C, C++, Java, JavaScript, and Python.

### Recursive Functions in C and C++

C and C++ support recursive functions, which can be used to solve problems like calculating factorial, generating Fibonacci sequences, or traversing tree structures.

*Factorial Calculation*

Here's an example of a recursive function to calculate the factorial of a number in C:

```c
#include <stdio.h>

int factorial(int n) {
    if (n <= 1) {
        return 1;
    } else {
        return n * factorial(n - 1);
```

```c
    }
}

int main() {
    int num = 5;
    printf("Factorial of %d is %d\n", num, factorial(num));
    return 0;
}
```

This code defines a `factorial` function that calls itself recursively until n becomes 1. It calculates the factorial of the given number.

*Recursive Fibonacci*

Another classic example is generating the Fibonacci sequence using recursion in C:

```c
#include <stdio.h>

int fibonacci(int n) {
    if (n <= 1) {
        return n;
    } else {
        return fibonacci(n - 1) + fibonacci(n - 2);
    }
}

int main() {
    int num = 6;
    printf("Fibonacci sequence up to %d terms:\n", num);
    for (int i = 0; i < num; i++) {
        printf("%d ", fibonacci(i));
    }
    printf("\n");
    return 0;
}
```

This code defines a `fibonacci` function that calls itself to calculate Fibonacci numbers recursively.

*Recursive Functions in Java*

Java also supports recursive functions. Let's look at a few examples.

*Binary Search*

Binary search can be implemented using recursion in Java:

```java
public class BinarySearch {
    public static int binarySearch(int[] arr, int target, int left, int right) {
        if (left <= right) {
```

```java
            int mid = left + (right - left) / 2;
            if (arr[mid] == target) {
                return mid;
            }
            if (arr[mid] < target) {
                return binarySearch(arr, target, mid + 1, right);
            } else {
                return binarySearch(arr, target, left, mid - 1);
            }
        }
        return -1;
    }

    public static void main(String[] args) {
        int[] arr = {1, 2, 3, 4, 5, 6, 7, 8, 9, 10};
        int target = 5;
        int result = binarySearch(arr, target, 0, arr.length - 1);
        if (result != -1) {
            System.out.println("Element found at index " + result);
        } else {
            System.out.println("Element not found");
        }
    }
}
```

This Java code demonstrates a recursive binary search algorithm to find an element in a sorted array.

## Recursive Functions in JavaScript

JavaScript is well-suited for recursive functions due to its dynamic nature. Here's an example of a recursive function to calculate factorial in JavaScript:

```javascript
function factorial(n) {
    if (n <= 1) {
        return 1;
    } else {
        return n * factorial(n - 1);
    }
}

const num = 5;
console.log(`Factorial of ${num} is ${factorial(num)}`);
```

JavaScript also allows recursion for tree traversal, nested data structures, and various other algorithms.

### Recursive Functions in Python

Python supports recursion and makes it easy to implement recursive functions. Here's an example of a recursive function to calculate the factorial of a number:

```python
def factorial(n):
    if n <= 1:
        return 1
    else:
        return n * factorial(n - 1)

num = 5
print(f"Factorial of {num} is {factorial(num)}")
```

Python's simplicity and readability make it an excellent choice for implementing recursive algorithms.

Recursion is a powerful technique, but it should be used judiciously. It's essential to have a base case to ensure that recursive calls eventually terminate. Recursive functions can be elegant and concise solutions for certain problems, but they may consume additional memory due to the function call stack. Understanding when and how to use recursion is crucial for efficient and maintainable code.

## 9.4 Exception Handling and Flow Control

Exception handling is a crucial aspect of programming that allows developers to handle unexpected situations or errors gracefully. In this section, we will explore how different programming languages handle exceptions and flow control.

### Exception Handling in C++

C++ uses a robust exception handling mechanism that allows developers to catch and handle exceptions using try, catch, and throw keywords.

```cpp
#include <iostream>
#include <stdexcept>

int main() {
    try {
        int x = 10;
        int y = 0;
        if (y == 0) {
            throw std::runtime_error("Division by zero is not allowed.");
        }
        int result = x / y;
        std::cout << "Result: " << result << std::endl;
    } catch (const std::exception& e) {
```

```cpp
        std::cerr << "Exception: " << e.what() << std::endl;
    }
    return 0;
}
```

In this C++ code, we attempt to perform division by zero, which is not allowed. An exception is thrown, and we catch it using a catch block. The program continues executing after handling the exception.

Exception Handling in Java

Java also provides robust exception handling with try, catch, and throw keywords.

```java
public class ExceptionHandlingExample {
    public static void main(String[] args) {
        try {
            int x = 10;
            int y = 0;
            if (y == 0) {
                throw new ArithmeticException("Division by zero is not allowe
d.");
            }
            int result = x / y;
            System.out.println("Result: " + result);
        } catch (ArithmeticException e) {
            System.err.println("Exception: " + e.getMessage());
        }
    }
}
```

This Java code demonstrates handling an ArithmeticException by throwing and catching it.

Exception Handling in JavaScript

JavaScript uses a different approach to handle exceptions, relying on the try, catch, and finally blocks.

```javascript
try {
    let x = 10;
    let y = 0;
    if (y === 0) {
        throw new Error("Division by zero is not allowed.");
    }
    let result = x / y;
    console.log("Result: " + result);
} catch (error) {
    console.error("Exception: " + error.message);
} finally {
    console.log("Execution completed.");
}
```

In this JavaScript code, we use `try`, `catch`, and `finally` to handle exceptions and ensure that the `finally` block is executed, regardless of whether an exception occurred.

## Exception Handling in Python

Python offers a straightforward and clean way to handle exceptions using `try` and `except` blocks.

```python
try:
    x = 10
    y = 0
    if y == 0:
        raise ZeroDivisionError("Division by zero is not allowed.")
    result = x / y
    print("Result:", result)
except ZeroDivisionError as e:
    print("Exception:", e)
```

This Python code demonstrates handling a `ZeroDivisionError` by raising and catching it using `try` and `except`.

Exception handling is essential for writing robust and reliable code. It allows developers to anticipate and manage errors, improving the overall quality of software. Each programming language has its own way of dealing with exceptions, but the fundamental principles of identifying, handling, and possibly propagating errors are consistent across languages. Proper exception handling contributes to code resilience and user satisfaction.

---

## 9.5 Writing Efficient and Effective Control Structures

In the world of programming, writing efficient and effective control structures is crucial for optimizing code performance and maintaining code readability. Control structures, including conditional statements and loops, govern the flow of a program and determine which code blocks are executed under different conditions. In this section, we will explore best practices and strategies for crafting control structures that strike a balance between performance and maintainability.

### Optimizing Conditional Statements

Conditional statements, such as `if`, `else if`, and `else`, are used to make decisions in code. Optimizing them involves ensuring that the most likely conditions are checked first, reducing the number of unnecessary checks. This practice is known as "short-circuiting" and can significantly improve code execution speed.

```python
# Inefficient
if condition1:
    # Code for condition1
```

```
elif condition2:
    # Code for condition2

# More efficient (if condition1 is more likely)
if condition1:
    # Code for condition1
else:
    # Code for condition2
```

By ordering conditions based on likelihood, you reduce the number of checks the program has to perform.

## Loop Optimization

Loops are essential for repetitive tasks, and optimizing them can lead to substantial performance improvements. One common technique is loop unrolling, where you manually expand the loop body to reduce loop control overhead.

```
// Loop unrolling in C
for (int i = 0; i < 10; i += 2) {
    // Loop body for i
    // Loop body for i+1
}
```

Another optimization strategy is loop fusion, where you combine multiple loops into one to minimize memory access and overhead.

## Avoiding Nested Loops

Nested loops can quickly lead to code complexity and reduced performance. Whenever possible, consider alternatives such as using dictionaries or sets for lookup operations instead of nested loops.

```
# Nested loops
for item1 in list1:
    for item2 in list2:
        if item1 == item2:
            # Perform some operation

# Alternative using sets
set1 = set(list1)
set2 = set(list2)
common_items = set1.intersection(set2)
for item in common_items:
    # Perform some operation
```

## Using Break and Continue Judiciously

The break and continue statements are powerful tools for control flow, but they should be used judiciously. Overusing them can make code less readable and harder to maintain.

Consider alternative control structures or refactoring code to reduce the need for these statements.

## Regular Code Reviews and Profiling

Regular code reviews by peers and profiling tools can help identify performance bottlenecks in control structures. Profilers provide insights into which parts of your code consume the most resources, helping you focus optimization efforts where they matter most.

## Choosing the Right Data Structures

The choice of data structures can impact the efficiency of your control structures. For example, using a hash map for fast lookups or a priority queue for sorting can improve algorithm efficiency.

In conclusion, writing efficient and effective control structures is essential for optimizing code performance and maintainability. By following best practices, optimizing conditional statements and loops, avoiding excessive nesting, and using tools like profilers, you can create code that not only runs faster but is also easier to maintain and debug. Remember that optimization should be guided by profiling results and not premature optimization, as it can lead to code complexity without significant benefits.

# Chapter 10: Object-Oriented Programming Across Languages

## 10.1 Core Concepts of OOP: Encapsulation, Inheritance, Polymorphism

Object-Oriented Programming (OOP) is a programming paradigm that focuses on organizing code into objects, which can encapsulate both data and behavior. OOP is not tied to a specific programming language but is a concept applied across many modern languages, including C++, Java, Python, and more. In this section, we will delve into the core concepts of OOP, namely Encapsulation, Inheritance, and Polymorphism.

### 1. Encapsulation

Encapsulation is the concept of bundling data (attributes) and methods (functions) that operate on that data into a single unit called an object. It aims to hide the internal implementation details of an object and provide a well-defined interface for interacting with it. Encapsulation helps in achieving data abstraction and modularity.

In most OOP languages, you create classes to define objects and their behaviors. Here's an example in Python:

```python
class Circle:
    def __init__(self, radius):
        self.radius = radius

    def area(self):
        return 3.14 * self.radius * self.radius
```

In this example, the `Circle` class encapsulates the `radius` attribute and the `area` method.

### 2. Inheritance

Inheritance is a mechanism that allows you to define a new class (subclass or derived class) based on an existing class (superclass or base class). The subclass inherits the attributes and methods of the superclass and can extend or override them. Inheritance promotes code reuse and hierarchical organization.

```java
class Animal {
    void speak() {
        System.out.println("Animal speaks");
    }
}

class Dog extends Animal {
    @Override
    void speak() {
        System.out.println("Dog barks");
    }
}
```

In this Java example, the Dog class inherits the speak method from the Animal class and provides its own implementation.

## 3. Polymorphism

Polymorphism is the ability of different classes to be treated as instances of their common base class. It allows you to write code that can work with objects of different classes in a consistent way. Polymorphism is often achieved through method overriding and interfaces.

In Python:

```python
class Shape:
    def area(self):
        pass

class Circle(Shape):
    def __init__(self, radius):
        self.radius = radius

    def area(self):
        return 3.14 * self.radius * self.radius

class Square(Shape):
    def __init__(self, side):
        self.side = side

    def area(self):
        return self.side * self.side
```

In this example, both Circle and Square are treated as instances of the Shape class when calculating their areas.

These core concepts of OOP provide a foundation for building complex and modular software systems. They enhance code reusability, maintainability, and flexibility, making OOP languages popular in various domains of software development. In the upcoming sections, we will explore how these concepts are implemented in specific programming languages and their real-world applications.

## 10.2 Comparing OOP in C++, Java, and Python

Object-Oriented Programming (OOP) is a versatile paradigm used in various programming languages. In this section, we'll compare how OOP is implemented in three popular languages: C++, Java, and Python. Each of these languages has its own syntax and features for implementing OOP principles.

C++ is known for its strong support for OOP. It provides features like classes, objects, inheritance, polymorphism, and encapsulation. Here's a brief overview of OOP in C++:

- **Classes and Objects**: C++ allows you to define classes and create objects. A class is a blueprint for objects, and objects are instances of classes.

- **Inheritance**: C++ supports single and multiple inheritance, allowing a class to inherit properties and behaviors from one or more base classes.

- **Polymorphism**: C++ supports both compile-time and runtime polymorphism. Compile-time polymorphism is achieved through function overloading, while runtime polymorphism is achieved using virtual functions.

- **Encapsulation**: C++ provides access specifiers (public, private, protected) to control the visibility of class members, achieving encapsulation.

```cpp
class Shape {
public:
    virtual double area() const = 0;
};

class Circle : public Shape {
private:
    double radius;
public:
    Circle(double r) : radius(r) {}
    double area() const override {
        return 3.14 * radius * radius;
    }
};

int main() {
    Circle c(5.0);
    Shape* s = &c;
    double result = s->area(); // Polymorphic call
    return 0;
}
```

Java

Java is a widely-used language for building object-oriented applications. Here's an overview of OOP in Java:

- **Classes and Objects**: Java follows a strict class-based model, where everything is defined in classes. Objects are instances of classes.

- **Inheritance**: Java supports single inheritance for classes but allows multiple inheritance through interfaces. All classes in Java implicitly inherit from the `Object` class.

- **Polymorphism**: Java achieves runtime polymorphism through method overriding. You can use the `@Override` annotation to indicate that a method overrides a superclass method.

- **Encapsulation**: Java uses access modifiers (public, private, protected) to control the visibility of class members, ensuring encapsulation.

```java
abstract class Shape {
    abstract double area();
}

class Circle extends Shape {
    private double radius;
    Circle(double r) {
        radius = r;
    }
    double area() {
        return 3.14 * radius * radius;
    }
}

public class Main {
    public static void main(String[] args) {
        Circle c = new Circle(5.0);
        Shape s = c; // Polymorphic assignment
        double result = s.area(); // Polymorphic call
    }
}
```

Python

Python is a dynamically-typed language that promotes simplicity and readability. It offers a different approach to OOP:

- **Classes and Objects**: Python supports classes and objects like C++ and Java, but it's more flexible due to its dynamic nature.

- **Inheritance**: Python supports single inheritance and multiple inheritance. It uses method resolution order (MRO) to determine the order of method invocation in case of multiple inheritance conflicts.

- **Polymorphism**: Polymorphism in Python is achieved through duck typing, allowing objects of different types to be used interchangeably if they support the required methods or attributes.

- **Encapsulation**: Python doesn't have strict access control mechanisms like C++ or Java. It follows the principle of "we are all consenting adults here," trusting developers to follow conventions for encapsulation.

```python
class Shape:
    def area(self):
        pass

class Circle(Shape):
    def __init__(self, radius):
        self.radius = radius

    def area(self):
        return 3.14 * self.radius * self.radius

c = Circle(5.0)
s = c  # Polymorphic assignment
result = s.area()   # Polymorphic call
```

Each of these languages has its own strengths and trade-offs when it comes to implementing OOP principles. The choice of language depends on the specific requirements of a project and the programming paradigm that best suits the problem at hand.

---

## 10.3 Design Patterns and Best Practices

Design patterns are reusable solutions to common software design problems. They provide a structured way to solve problems and improve code maintainability. In this section, we'll discuss design patterns and best practices in C++, Java, and Python.

C++

C++ supports various design patterns, and it encourages developers to follow best practices for memory management and performance. Some popular design patterns in C++ include:

- **Singleton Pattern**: Ensures a class has only one instance and provides a global point of access to it. It's useful for managing resources like database connections.

- **Factory Pattern**: Provides an interface for creating objects but lets subclasses alter the type of objects that will be created. It's commonly used for creating objects with different implementations.

- **Observer Pattern**: Defines a one-to-many dependency between objects so that when one object changes state, all its dependents are notified and updated automatically.

C++ best practices include using smart pointers (e.g., std::shared_ptr, std::unique_ptr) for memory management, following the RAII (Resource Acquisition Is Initialization) principle, and using the Standard Template Library (STL) for containers and algorithms.

## Java

Java has a rich set of design patterns and encourages developers to follow object-oriented principles. Some well-known design patterns in Java include:

- **Singleton Pattern**: Java provides an easy way to implement a thread-safe singleton using the Enum or static final field approach.

- **Factory Pattern**: Java encourages the use of interfaces and abstract classes for creating families of related objects. The factory pattern is commonly used in Java.

- **Observer Pattern**: Java provides built-in support for the observer pattern through the java.util.Observable class and java.util.Observer interface.

Java best practices include using proper exception handling, following naming conventions, using interfaces to define contracts, and leveraging Java's extensive standard library.

## Python

Python promotes simplicity and readability, and it has its own way of implementing design patterns. Some design patterns and best practices in Python include:

- **Singleton Pattern**: Python's modules are singletons by default. You can create a singleton class by overriding the __new__ method.

- **Factory Pattern**: Python uses functions and classes to create objects. You can use functions as factories to create objects of different types.

- **Observer Pattern**: Python provides a simple way to implement the observer pattern using built-in decorators or custom event handling mechanisms.

Python best practices include following PEP 8 style guidelines, using context managers (with statements) for resource management, and preferring duck typing and composition over inheritance.

Remember that design patterns should be used judiciously and not forced into every situation. The choice of a design pattern should align with the specific requirements of your project and the principles of good software design. Additionally, adhering to language-specific best practices ensures that your code is maintainable, readable, and follows community conventions.

## 10.4 The Impact of OOP on Software Development

Object-Oriented Programming (OOP) has had a profound impact on software development over the years. It introduced a new way of thinking about and organizing code, which has led to more maintainable, modular, and reusable software. In this section, we'll explore the significant impact of OOP on software development.

### Encapsulation and Modularity

OOP encourages encapsulation, which means bundling data (attributes) and the methods (functions) that operate on that data into a single unit known as a class. This concept helps in creating modular code where each class is responsible for a specific part of the functionality. This modularity makes it easier to understand and maintain large codebases.

```java
// Java example demonstrating encapsulation
public class Employee {
    private String name;
    private double salary;

    public Employee(String name, double salary) {
        this.name = name;
        this.salary = salary;
    }

    public void increaseSalary(double amount) {
        if (amount > 0) {
            this.salary += amount;
        }
    }
}
```

### Inheritance and Code Reuse

Inheritance, a fundamental OOP concept, allows a class to inherit properties and behaviors from another class. This promotes code reuse by enabling developers to create new classes based on existing ones. Inheritance facilitates the creation of hierarchies and promotes the DRY (Don't Repeat Yourself) principle.

```python
# Python example demonstrating inheritance
class Animal:
    def __init__(self, name):
        self.name = name

    def speak(self):
        pass

class Dog(Animal):
    def speak(self):
        return "Woof!"
```

```
class Cat(Animal):
    def speak(self):
        return "Meow!"
```

Polymorphism and Flexibility

Polymorphism allows objects of different classes to be treated as objects of a common base class. This concept provides flexibility by allowing different implementations of methods to be invoked based on the actual type of the object at runtime. Polymorphism is crucial for writing generic code and designing extensible systems.

```
// C++ example demonstrating polymorphism
class Shape {
public:
    virtual double area() const = 0;
};

class Circle : public Shape {
private:
    double radius;

public:
    Circle(double radius) : radius(radius) {}

    double area() const override {
        return 3.14 * radius * radius;
    }
};
```

Encapsulation of State and Behavior

OOP aligns well with real-world modeling by encapsulating an object's state (attributes) and behavior (methods) together. This modeling approach makes it intuitive to represent entities and their interactions in software, making it easier to communicate and collaborate during development.

Software Design Patterns

OOP introduced numerous design patterns that are widely adopted in software development. These patterns provide reusable solutions to common problems and help maintain high-quality code. Examples include the Singleton, Factory, and Observer patterns.

Challenges and Criticisms

While OOP has many advantages, it's not without challenges and criticisms. It can lead to complex class hierarchies, which may become difficult to maintain. Overuse of inheritance can lead to tight coupling, making code less flexible. Additionally, some developers argue that OOP is not always the best paradigm for all types of software.

In conclusion, Object-Oriented Programming has had a significant impact on software development by promoting encapsulation, modularity, code reuse, flexibility, and design patterns. While it's not a one-size-fits-all solution, understanding and using OOP principles appropriately can lead to well-structured and maintainable software.

---

## 10.5 Challenges and Criticisms of OOP

Object-Oriented Programming (OOP) is a widely adopted programming paradigm with many advantages, as discussed in previous sections. However, it's not without its challenges and criticisms. In this section, we'll explore some of the common challenges and criticisms associated with OOP.

### Complex Class Hierarchies

One of the challenges of OOP is the potential for complex class hierarchies. As software projects grow, the number of classes and their relationships can become overwhelming. This complexity can make it challenging to understand, navigate, and maintain the codebase.

```
// Example of a complex class hierarchy
class Animal { /* ... */ }
class Mammal extends Animal { /* ... */ }
class Reptile extends Animal { /* ... */ }
class Bird extends Animal { /* ... */ }
class Dog extends Mammal { /* ... */ }
class Cat extends Mammal { /* ... */ }
class Snake extends Reptile { /* ... */ }
class Parrot extends Bird { /* ... */ }
```

### Tight Coupling

Inheritance, a fundamental concept in OOP, can lead to tight coupling between classes. Tight coupling means that changes in one class can have a cascading effect on other classes, making the code less flexible and more challenging to maintain. Overuse of inheritance can exacerbate this problem.

```python
# Example of tight coupling through inheritance
class Shape:
    def area(self):
        pass

class Circle(Shape):
    def area(self):
        return 3.14 * self.radius * self.radius

class Rectangle(Shape):
```

```python
    def area(self):
        return self.width * self.height
```

## Overhead and Performance

OOP can introduce some overhead in terms of memory and processing power. Objects typically carry additional information beyond their actual data (e.g., vtables for method dispatch in C++), which can impact performance, especially in resource-constrained environments.

```cpp
// C++ example showing vtable overhead
class Shape {
public:
    virtual double area() const = 0;
};

class Circle : public Shape {
private:
    double radius;

public:
    Circle(double radius) : radius(radius) {}

    double area() const override {
        return 3.14 * radius * radius;
    }
};
```

## Difficulty in Learning

OOP can be more challenging for beginners to grasp compared to other programming paradigms. The concept of objects, classes, inheritance, and polymorphism can be abstract and require a different way of thinking. This learning curve can slow down the development process for those new to OOP.

## Not Always the Best Fit

OOP is not always the best fit for every software project. Some systems may have characteristics that make other paradigms, such as procedural or functional programming, more suitable. Trying to force an OOP approach in such cases can lead to unnecessary complexity.

In conclusion, while OOP has many advantages and has significantly influenced software development, it's essential to be aware of its challenges and criticisms. Developers should carefully consider whether OOP is the right choice for a given project and use its principles judiciously to avoid common pitfalls like complex hierarchies and tight coupling.

# Chapter 11: Functional Programming: A Paradigm Shift

## Section 11.1: Introduction to Functional Programming

Functional programming is a programming paradigm that treats computation as the evaluation of mathematical functions and avoids changing-state and mutable data. It has gained popularity in recent years due to its elegant and concise coding style, which often leads to more maintainable and bug-free code.

At its core, functional programming revolves around the concept of functions as first-class citizens. In functional languages, functions can be assigned to variables, passed as arguments, and returned as values. This higher-order function capability is one of the key distinguishing features of functional programming languages.

One fundamental concept in functional programming is immutability. In functional languages, once data is assigned, it cannot be modified. Instead, new data is created with each transformation. This immutability ensures that data remains unchanged, reducing the chances of side effects and making the code more predictable.

Functional programming languages often include features like pattern matching and higher-order functions, which simplify code and make it more expressive. These languages also encourage recursion as a primary means of repetition, which can be more elegant than traditional loops for certain problems.

### Advantages of Functional Programming

Functional programming offers several advantages:

1. **Conciseness:** Functional code is often more concise and expressive than equivalent imperative code. This can lead to faster development and easier maintenance.

2. **Predictability:** Immutability and absence of side effects make functional programs more predictable and easier to reason about.

3. **Parallelism:** Functional programming encourages pure functions, which can be easily parallelized, taking advantage of multi-core processors.

4. **Reusability:** Functional code tends to be more modular, making it easier to reuse functions in various parts of the codebase.

5. **Testing:** Functional code is typically easier to test since it relies on pure functions with well-defined inputs and outputs.

### Functional Features in Python and JavaScript

While languages like Haskell and Lisp are known for their pure functional approach, mainstream languages like Python and JavaScript also support functional programming to varying degrees.

In Python, you can use functions like map, filter, and reduce to work with lists in a functional style. Python also supports list comprehensions, which allow for concise iteration and transformation of lists.

JavaScript, on the other hand, has features like anonymous functions, closures, and first-class functions that make it conducive to functional programming. Libraries like Underscore.js and lodash provide utility functions for functional-style programming in JavaScript.

Functional programming is not an all-or-nothing choice; you can choose to incorporate functional principles into your code as needed, even in languages that are not purely functional.

In the next sections, we'll delve deeper into specific functional features and use cases in Python and JavaScript, exploring how functional programming can enhance your coding skills and problem-solving abilities.

---

## Section 11.2: Functional Features in Python and JavaScript

Functional programming concepts are not limited to purely functional languages like Haskell; they can be applied effectively in mainstream languages such as Python and JavaScript. In this section, we will explore some of the functional features and techniques available in these languages.

### Python and Functional Programming

Python supports a variety of functional programming features and constructs that allow developers to write more concise and expressive code.

1. **Lambda Functions:** Python allows the creation of anonymous functions using the lambda keyword. These functions are often used as arguments to higher-order functions like map, filter, and reduce.

```python
square = lambda x: x ** 2
result = list(map(square, [1, 2, 3, 4, 5]))   # [1, 4, 9, 16, 25]
```

2. **Map, Filter, and Reduce:** These built-in functions enable functional-style operations on sequences like lists. map applies a function to each element, filter selects elements based on a condition, and reduce aggregates elements.

```python
# Using map to double each element
numbers = [1, 2, 3, 4]
doubled = list(map(lambda x: x * 2, numbers))   # [2, 4, 6, 8]

# Using filter to select even numbers
even = list(filter(lambda x: x % 2 == 0, numbers))   # [2, 4]
```

```python
# Using reduce to find the sum of elements
from functools import reduce
total = reduce(lambda x, y: x + y, numbers)  # 10
```

3. **List Comprehensions:** Python's list comprehensions provide a concise way to create lists based on existing ones, often eliminating the need for explicit loops.

```python
squares = [x ** 2 for x in range(1, 6)]  # [1, 4, 9, 16, 25]
```

4. **Immutable Data Structures:** Python's tuples and frozensets are immutable data structures, which align with functional programming principles. Once created, their values cannot be changed.

```python
point = (3, 4)
```

## JavaScript and Functional Programming

JavaScript's support for functional programming is deeply ingrained in its design, with features that encourage functional coding practices.

1. **First-Class Functions:** In JavaScript, functions are first-class citizens, meaning they can be assigned to variables, passed as arguments, and returned as values. This enables the use of higher-order functions.

```javascript
const square = x => x ** 2;
const result = [1, 2, 3, 4, 5].map(square); // [1, 4, 9, 16, 25]
```

2. **Closures:** JavaScript closures allow functions to capture and remember their surrounding lexical scope. This is useful for creating private variables and data encapsulation.

```javascript
function makeCounter() {
  let count = 0;
  return () => {
    count++;
    return count;
  };
}
const counter = makeCounter();
console.log(counter()); // 1
console.log(counter()); // 2
```

3. **Higher-Order Functions:** JavaScript has a rich set of higher-order functions like map, filter, and reduce that make it easy to work with arrays in a functional manner.

```javascript
const numbers = [1, 2, 3, 4];
const doubled = numbers.map(x => x * 2); // [2, 4, 6, 8]
```

```javascript
const even = numbers.filter(x => x % 2 === 0); // [2, 4]
const total = numbers.reduce((x, y) => x + y, 0); // 10
```

4.  **Immutability:** While JavaScript's objects are mutable, libraries like Immutable.js provide immutable data structures, promoting functional programming practices.

```javascript
const { Map } = require("immutable");
const map1 = Map({ a: 1, b: 2 });
const map2 = map1.set("b", 3);
```

Both Python and JavaScript offer powerful tools for functional programming, making it possible to write cleaner, more modular, and often more efficient code. By embracing functional principles, developers can write code that is easier to reason about and maintain, ultimately leading to higher-quality software.

---

## Section 11.3: Comparing Imperative and Functional Approaches

In this section, we will explore the differences between imperative and functional programming approaches and understand when each approach is most suitable.

### Imperative Programming

Imperative programming is a style of coding that focuses on describing the **steps** necessary to achieve a specific goal. It is often characterized by the use of statements that change program **state**. In an imperative program, you specify the **how** of solving a problem, detailing every action required to reach the desired outcome.

```python
# An imperative Python function to calculate the sum of squares of numbers from 1 to n.
def sum_of_squares(n):
    total = 0
    for i in range(1, n + 1):
        total += i ** 2
    return total
```

The above code demonstrates an imperative approach to calculating the sum of squares. It explicitly defines a loop and accumulates the result step by step.

### Functional Programming

Functional programming, on the other hand, emphasizes **what** needs to be done rather than **how** to do it. It treats computation as the evaluation of mathematical functions and avoids changing state and mutable data. Functional code tends to be more concise, modular, and easier to reason about.

```python
# A functional Python implementation using a higher-order function.
def sum_of_squares(n):
    return sum(map(lambda x: x ** 2, range(1, n + 1)))
```

In the functional approach, we use the map and sum functions to express the computation more declaratively. We don't specify the individual steps; instead, we describe the transformation to be applied to the data.

### When to Choose Each Approach

The choice between imperative and functional programming depends on the problem and the context:

- **Imperative** programming is often more suitable for tasks that involve complex state changes, mutable data structures, and low-level operations. It can be a better choice when performance or resource utilization is a critical concern.

- **Functional** programming shines when you want to emphasize simplicity, maintainability, and correctness. It is particularly effective for tasks that involve data transformation, filtering, or aggregation, as it encourages a more declarative and less error-prone style of coding.

In practice, many modern programming languages, including Python and JavaScript, allow you to mix imperative and functional approaches. This flexibility enables developers to choose the most appropriate paradigm for each specific part of their codebase.

It's essential to strike a balance and choose the approach that best matches the problem's nature and the project's requirements. This flexibility can lead to codebases that are both efficient and maintainable.

---

## Section 11.4: Use Cases for Functional Programming

Functional programming (FP) is a paradigm with distinct characteristics that make it suitable for certain types of problems. In this section, we will explore common use cases where FP shines.

### 1. Data Transformation and Processing

Functional programming is well-suited for tasks that involve data transformation, filtering, and aggregation. Operations like map, filter, and reduce are staples in functional programming languages and libraries, making it easy to manipulate data in a clean and concise manner.

```python
# Using functional programming to manipulate a list of numbers.
numbers = [1, 2, 3, 4, 5]
# Calculate the squares of all numbers greater than 2.
```

```python
squares = list(map(lambda x: x ** 2, filter(lambda x: x > 2, numbers)))
# Result: [9, 16, 25]
```

## 2. Parallel and Concurrent Programming

FP's emphasis on immutability and statelessness makes it an excellent choice for parallel and concurrent programming. Because functions are isolated and don't modify shared state, it's easier to reason about and manage concurrency.

```python
# Using functional programming with Python's multiprocessing library.
from multiprocessing import Pool

def square(x):
    return x ** 2

if __name__ == '__main__':
    numbers = [1, 2, 3, 4, 5]
    with Pool() as pool:
        squares = pool.map(square, numbers)
    # Result: [1, 4, 9, 16, 25]
```

## 3. Complex Mathematical Calculations

Functional programming languages, especially those with strong support for first-class functions, excel in solving mathematical problems. FP's mathematical foundation allows for concise and expressive representations of complex mathematical functions and algorithms.

```haskell
-- A simple Haskell function to calculate the factorial of a number.
factorial :: Integer -> Integer
factorial 0 = 1
factorial n = n * factorial (n - 1)
```

## 4. Handling Streams and Events

In event-driven or reactive programming, where streams of data and events are common, FP concepts are valuable. Libraries like RxJS in JavaScript and reactive frameworks leverage functional programming principles to handle asynchronous data flows.

```javascript
// Using RxJS to filter and map values in an observable stream.
import { from } from 'rxjs';
import { filter, map } from 'rxjs/operators';

const numbers = from([1, 2, 3, 4, 5]);
const squares = numbers.pipe(
    filter(x => x > 2),
    map(x => x ** 2)
);
// Result: 9, 16, 25 (as an observable)
```

## 5. Domain-Specific Languages (DSLs)

Functional programming is often used to create domain-specific languages (DSLs) tailored to specific problem domains. DSLs enable developers to write code that closely resembles the problem space, improving readability and maintainability.

```
-- An example of a DSL for working with financial transactions in Haskell.
transfer :: Account -> Account -> Amount -> Transaction
transfer fromAccount toAccount amount =
    Transaction fromAccount toAccount (negate amount) :+ Transaction toAccoun
t fromAccount amount
```

Functional programming's suitability for these use cases arises from its emphasis on immutability, purity, and the absence of side effects. While not all problems are best solved with FP, recognizing when to apply its principles can lead to cleaner, more maintainable code in specific scenarios.

---

## Section 11.5: The Future of Functional Programming

Functional programming (FP) has been gaining traction in recent years, and its future looks promising. Here, we'll discuss some trends and developments that indicate the continued relevance and growth of FP.

### 1. Wider Adoption in Mainstream Languages

Many mainstream programming languages have been incorporating functional programming features. Languages like Python, JavaScript, and C# have introduced functional constructs, making it easier for developers to adopt FP principles without switching to purely functional languages.

```
# Python's introduction of lambda functions and comprehensions.
squares = [x ** 2 for x in range(1, 6)]
# Result: [1, 4, 9, 16, 25]
```

### 2. Functional-First Languages

Functional-first languages like Haskell, Elm, and Clojure continue to thrive. They provide strong support for FP principles and are chosen for projects that require correctness, reliability, and maintainability.

```
-- A simple Haskell function that reverses a list.
reverseList :: [a] -> [a]
reverseList [] = []
reverseList (x:xs) = reverseList xs ++ [x]
```

### 3. Reactive and Event-Driven Systems

With the rise of reactive and event-driven architectures, functional programming is becoming more relevant. Libraries and frameworks like Akka for Scala and RxJS for JavaScript enable developers to build highly responsive and scalable systems using FP concepts.

```scala
// Using Akka Streams for event-driven processing in Scala.
import akka.actor.ActorSystem
import akka.stream._
import akka.stream.scaladsl._

implicit val system: ActorSystem = ActorSystem("akka-streams-example")
implicit val materializer: Materializer = ActorMaterializer()

val numbers = Source(1 to 5)
val squares = numbers.map(x => x * x)
// Result: 1, 4, 9, 16, 25 (as a stream)
```

### 4. Advances in Type Systems

Type systems in functional languages are becoming more sophisticated, enabling better type inference and safer code. Features like dependent types, refined types, and gradual typing are emerging, enhancing the expressiveness and correctness of FP code.

```elm
-- An Elm type alias representing positive integers.
type alias PositiveInt = Int
    |> where (\x -> x > 0)
```

### 5. Functional for Data Science and AI

Functional programming is finding applications in data science and artificial intelligence. Libraries like TensorFlow for Python offer functional APIs for deep learning, and functional languages like Scala are used for distributed data processing in big data environments.

```python
# Functional API in TensorFlow for deep learning.
import tensorflow as tf

model = tf.keras.Sequential([
    tf.keras.layers.Dense(128, activation='relu'),
    tf.keras.layers.Dense(10, activation='softmax')
])
```

### 6. Functional in Blockchain and Smart Contracts

Blockchain platforms like Ethereum are embracing functional languages like Solidity for writing smart contracts. FP's deterministic and verifiable nature aligns well with the requirements of blockchain systems.

```solidity
// A simple smart contract in Solidity.
pragma solidity ^0.8.0;
```

```
contract SimpleStorage {
    uint256 storedData;

    function set(uint256 x) public {
        storedData = x;
    }

    function get() public view returns (uint256) {
        return storedData;
    }
}
```

The future of functional programming is not limited to these trends alone. As software development continues to evolve, FP's principles of immutability, purity, and composability are expected to play a significant role in addressing the challenges of modern software engineering, making it a valuable skill for developers to learn and master.

# Chapter 12: Memory Management Across Languages

## Section 12.1: Understanding Stack and Heap Allocation

Memory management is a critical aspect of programming languages, as it directly impacts the allocation and deallocation of memory during program execution. One fundamental concept in memory management is the distinction between stack and heap allocation.

### Stack Allocation

Stack memory is a region of memory that follows a last-in, first-out (LIFO) allocation scheme. It is typically used for storing local variables, function call information, and managing function execution. Stack allocation is fast and deterministic because memory is allocated and deallocated in a known order.

In languages like C and C++, when you declare a local variable inside a function, it is usually allocated on the stack.

```
void foo() {
    int x = 42; // 'x' is allocated on the stack
}
```

Stack memory is limited in size, and its scope is typically limited to the duration of a function call. When a function exits, the memory allocated on the stack for its local variables is automatically deallocated.

### Heap Allocation

Heap memory, on the other hand, is a region of memory used for dynamic memory allocation. It is not bound by the same LIFO constraints as the stack and is suitable for managing data structures of varying sizes and lifetimes. Heap memory is managed explicitly by the programmer, and it is essential to allocate and deallocate memory correctly to avoid memory leaks or access violations.

Languages like C and C++ provide functions like `malloc` and `free` for allocating and deallocating memory on the heap.

```
int *arr = (int *)malloc(5 * sizeof(int)); // Allocating an array on the heap
free(arr); // Deallocating the memory when no longer needed
```

Heap memory allows for dynamic memory allocation and can persist beyond the scope of a single function or block, making it suitable for data structures like linked lists, trees, and objects with complex lifetimes.

### Choosing Between Stack and Heap

The choice between stack and heap allocation depends on the requirements of your program:

- Use stack allocation for short-lived objects with a predictable lifetime.
- Use heap allocation for objects with a dynamic or longer lifetime.
- Be cautious when using heap memory, as manual management is required to prevent memory leaks.

Understanding the differences between stack and heap memory is crucial for writing efficient and robust programs. It also plays a significant role in the performance and reliability of software written in different programming languages.

## Section 12.2: Automatic vs Manual Memory Management

Memory management in programming languages can be categorized into two main approaches: automatic memory management (garbage collection) and manual memory management. Each approach has its advantages and disadvantages, and the choice between them often depends on the language's design goals and the programmer's preferences.

### Automatic Memory Management (Garbage Collection)

Automatic memory management, commonly referred to as garbage collection, is a memory management technique used by languages like Java, Python, C#, and JavaScript. In this approach, the language runtime system automatically tracks and reclaims memory that is no longer in use, relieving programmers from the responsibility of explicit memory allocation and deallocation.

Garbage collection uses algorithms to identify and collect memory that can no longer be accessed by the program. This includes memory occupied by objects that are no longer referenced, cyclic references, and other unreachable memory.

Here's a simplified example in Python:

```python
# Automatic memory management (Python)
def create_and_use_list():
    my_list = [1, 2, 3]   # List created
    print(my_list[0])     # List used

create_and_use_list()   # List goes out of scope and becomes eligible for gar
bage collection
```

In this example, when the create_and_use_list function completes, the my_list object goes out of scope, becomes unreachable, and is eventually garbage collected.

Automatic memory management helps prevent common memory-related bugs such as memory leaks and dangling pointers. However, it can introduce some runtime overhead due to the need for garbage collection algorithms, which may briefly pause program execution during collection.

## Manual Memory Management

Manual memory management requires programmers to explicitly allocate and deallocate memory. Languages like C and C++ rely on manual memory management, giving programmers fine-grained control over memory usage.

In languages with manual memory management, memory allocation is typically done using functions like `malloc` (allocate) and deallocation using `free` (deallocate). Programmers are responsible for ensuring that memory is properly allocated and deallocated, which can be error-prone but offers more predictable performance.

```
// Manual memory management (C)
int *arr = (int *)malloc(5 * sizeof(int)); // Memory allocation
free(arr); // Memory deallocation
```

Manual memory management can be efficient when done correctly, but it also presents challenges such as memory leaks, double frees, and dangling pointers. Programs written in languages with manual memory management require careful memory management practices to avoid these issues.

## Choosing Between Approaches

The choice between automatic and manual memory management depends on factors such as language design goals, programmer experience, and project requirements. Languages with automatic memory management are often chosen for productivity and safety, while languages with manual memory management are preferred for performance-critical applications and systems programming. Hybrid approaches, like those used in C++ with smart pointers, attempt to combine the benefits of both approaches.

---

## Section 12.3: Garbage Collection Mechanisms in Java and Python

Garbage collection is a critical aspect of memory management in modern programming languages. It helps prevent memory leaks and ensures that memory is efficiently reclaimed when it's no longer needed. In this section, we'll explore how garbage collection works in two popular languages: Java and Python.

### Garbage Collection in Java

Java employs automatic garbage collection to manage memory. It uses a combination of techniques to identify and reclaim unreachable objects. The most common garbage collection algorithm used in Java is the generational garbage collection.

In generational garbage collection, memory is divided into two main areas: the young generation and the old generation. New objects are allocated in the young generation. When the young generation fills up, a minor garbage collection is triggered to reclaim memory. Objects that survive multiple minor collections are eventually promoted to the old generation. Major garbage collections are less frequent and occur in the old generation.

Here's a simple example in Java:

```java
// Garbage collection in Java
class MyClass {
    public void finalize() {
        System.out.println("Object finalized");
    }
}

public class GarbageCollectionDemo {
    public static void main(String[] args) {
        MyClass obj1 = new MyClass();
        MyClass obj2 = new MyClass();
        obj1 = null; // Make obj1 eligible for garbage collection
        System.gc(); // Suggest JVM to run garbage collection
    }
}
```

In this example, we create two MyClass objects, and then we set obj1 to null to make it eligible for garbage collection. We then suggest the JVM to run garbage collection using System.gc(). When the JVM decides to collect garbage, it will call the finalize method of eligible objects before reclaiming their memory.

Garbage Collection in Python

Python also uses automatic garbage collection, but it employs a different mechanism. Python uses a reference counting technique combined with a cycle detector.

Reference counting keeps track of how many references point to an object. When an object's reference count drops to zero, it means the object is no longer accessible and can be safely reclaimed.

```python
# Garbage collection in Python
import gc

class MyClass:
    def __del__(self):
        print("Object finalized")

obj1 = MyClass()
obj2 = obj1   # Creating a reference to obj1
del obj1   # Decrease reference count of obj1

# Explicitly run garbage collection
gc.collect()
```

In this Python example, we create an instance of MyClass, create a reference to it with obj2, and then delete obj1. The reference count of the object decreases, and when we explicitly run gc.collect(), Python's garbage collector reclaims the memory.

Python's cycle detector is used to detect and break reference cycles when objects reference each other, ensuring that memory is properly released even in complex data structures.

Both Java and Python provide automatic memory management through garbage collection, relieving developers from manual memory allocation and deallocation, and reducing the risk of memory-related bugs. However, understanding the underlying mechanisms can help optimize memory usage and avoid common pitfalls.

## Section 12.4: Memory Leaks and Management in C and C++

Memory management in C and C++ is significantly different from languages with garbage collection like Java and Python. While it offers more control over memory, it also introduces the risk of memory leaks and undefined behavior if not handled properly.

### Memory Leaks in C and C++

In C and C++, developers have explicit control over memory allocation and deallocation using functions like malloc, calloc, realloc, and free. This control can lead to memory leaks when developers forget to deallocate memory explicitly. A memory leak occurs when allocated memory is no longer reachable but hasn't been freed, causing the program to consume increasing amounts of memory over time.

Here's an example in C that demonstrates a memory leak:

```c
#include <stdio.h>
#include <stdlib.h>

int main() {
    int *arr = (int *)malloc(5 * sizeof(int)); // Allocate memory for an inte
ger array

    if (arr == NULL) {
        perror("Memory allocation failed");
        return 1;
    }

    // Perform some operations with arr

    // Memory Leak: Forgot to free the allocated memory
    // free(arr);
```

```
    return 0;
}
```

In this example, memory is allocated for an integer array using `malloc`, but the code forgets to release the memory using `free`. This leads to a memory leak, as the allocated memory is never deallocated.

Management Strategies in C and C++

To manage memory effectively in C and C++, it's essential to follow best practices:

1. **Always Free Allocated Memory**: Ensure that every memory allocation using functions like `malloc` is paired with a corresponding `free` to release memory when it's no longer needed.

2. **Use Smart Pointers (C++)**: In C++, you can use smart pointers like `std::shared_ptr` and `std::unique_ptr` to automate memory management. They automatically release memory when it's no longer referenced, reducing the risk of memory leaks.

3. **Valgrind (C/C++)**: Tools like Valgrind can help detect memory leaks and other memory-related issues in C and C++ programs. Running your code through Valgrind during development can catch memory leaks early.

4. **RAII (Resource Acquisition Is Initialization)**: In C++, the RAII principle involves acquiring resources like memory in constructors and releasing them in destructors. RAII can help ensure that resources are automatically managed when objects go out of scope.

5. **Static Analysis Tools**: Use static analysis tools to analyze your code for potential memory leaks and undefined behavior.

Memory management in C and C++ requires diligence and careful attention to detail. While these languages offer greater control over memory, developers must be responsible for correctly allocating and deallocating memory to avoid leaks and ensure program stability.

---

Section 12.5: Best Practices for Efficient Memory Usage

Efficient memory usage is crucial in programming, as it directly impacts the performance and stability of your applications. In this section, we'll explore best practices for managing memory efficiently in various programming languages, with a focus on C and C++.

### 1. Use Stack Memory When Appropriate

Stack memory is faster to allocate and deallocate than heap memory. Use the stack for small, short-lived variables like local variables within functions. These variables are automatically released when they go out of scope, reducing the risk of memory leaks.

```
void exampleFunction() {
    int x = 5; // x is a stack variable
    // ...
} // x is automatically deallocated when the function exits
```

### 2. Limit Dynamic Memory Allocation

Dynamic memory allocation (e.g., using malloc or new) should be used judiciously. Frequent dynamic memory allocation and deallocation can lead to fragmentation and memory overhead. Instead, consider using fixed-size arrays or data structures when the maximum size is known.

### 3. Avoid Memory Leaks

Always release memory you've allocated when it's no longer needed. In C and C++, use free or delete. In languages with garbage collection, rely on the garbage collector to reclaim memory. Tools like Valgrind can help detect memory leaks during development.

### 4. Use RAII in C++

In C++, embrace the RAII (Resource Acquisition Is Initialization) principle. It involves acquiring and releasing resources within the constructors and destructors of objects. RAII ensures that resources, including memory, are properly managed when objects go out of scope.

```
class ResourceWrapper {
public:
    ResourceWrapper() {
        // Acquire resource, e.g., allocate memory
    }

    ~ResourceWrapper() {
        // Release resource, e.g., deallocate memory
    }
};
```

### 5. Employ Smart Pointers (C++)

In C++, prefer smart pointers like std::shared_ptr and std::unique_ptr over raw pointers. Smart pointers automate memory management, reducing the likelihood of memory leaks and ensuring timely deallocation.

```
std::shared_ptr<int> shared = std::make_shared<int>(42);
std::unique_ptr<int> unique = std::make_unique<int>(42);
```

## 6. Profile and Optimize

Use profiling tools to identify memory bottlenecks in your code. Profilers help pinpoint areas where memory is allocated excessively or inefficiently. Once identified, you can optimize memory usage accordingly.

## 7. Avoid Global Variables

Global variables can remain in memory throughout the program's execution, leading to unnecessary memory consumption. Minimize the use of global variables, and prefer local scope whenever possible.

## 8. Check Return Values of Allocation Functions

When allocating memory dynamically, always check the return values of allocation functions (e.g., `malloc`, `new`) to ensure they succeeded. Failing to do so can result in undefined behavior if allocation fails.

```
int *ptr = (int *)malloc(sizeof(int));
if (ptr == NULL) {
    // Allocation failed, handle the error
}
```

## 9. Release Resources in Error Handling Paths

When handling errors or exceptions, ensure that any allocated resources, including memory, are properly released. Failing to release resources in error paths can lead to resource leaks.

Efficient memory management is an essential skill for developers, regardless of the programming language they work with. By following these best practices, you can write code that not only conserves memory but also minimizes the risk of memory-related issues such as leaks and fragmentation, ultimately leading to more robust and performant software.

# Chapter 13: Concurrency and Parallelism

In this chapter, we delve into the fascinating world of concurrency and parallelism in programming. Concurrency and parallelism are essential concepts that enable a program to perform multiple tasks simultaneously, making efficient use of modern multi-core processors. We'll explore the basics of concurrency, multithreading, asynchronous programming, synchronization, and real-world applications of concurrent programming.

## Section 13.1: Basics of Concurrency and Parallelism

Concurrency and parallelism are often used interchangeably, but they represent distinct concepts in the world of programming:

### Concurrency

Concurrency refers to the ability of a program to manage multiple tasks seemingly simultaneously. It doesn't necessarily mean that tasks run in parallel, but it gives the illusion of overlapping execution. Concurrency is particularly useful in scenarios where tasks involve waiting for external events or resources.

For example, in a web server, multiple clients may request resources simultaneously. Concurrency allows the server to handle these requests without waiting for one to complete before starting the next.

### Parallelism

Parallelism involves the actual simultaneous execution of multiple tasks, usually leveraging multiple CPU cores or processors. Parallelism aims to achieve true simultaneous execution for performance improvement.

In parallel processing, tasks are divided into smaller subtasks, each of which can be executed concurrently on separate processors or cores. This can significantly speed up computations for tasks that are inherently parallelizable.

Let's look at a code snippet in Python that demonstrates a concurrent program using the threading module:

```python
import threading

def print_numbers():
    for i in range(1, 6):
        print(f"Number {i}")

def print_letters():
    for letter in 'abcde':
        print(f"Letter {letter}")

# Create two threads
```

```
thread1 = threading.Thread(target=print_numbers)
thread2 = threading.Thread(target=print_letters)

# Start the threads
thread1.start()
thread2.start()

# Wait for both threads to finish
thread1.join()
thread2.join()
```

In this example, two threads are created, each executing a different function concurrently.

Concurrency and parallelism are essential for improving program performance, responsiveness, and resource utilization. However, managing concurrent access to shared resources and handling synchronization are challenges that must be addressed to avoid issues like race conditions and deadlocks, which we'll explore further in later sections.

---

## Section 13.2: Multithreading in Java and C++

Multithreading is a powerful concept that allows programs to perform multiple tasks concurrently, making efficient use of modern hardware. In this section, we will explore multithreading in Java and C++, two popular programming languages known for their robust support for multithreaded applications.

### Java Multithreading

Java provides built-in support for multithreading through the java.lang.Thread class. To create a multithreaded application in Java, you typically follow these steps:

1.  Create a class that extends the Thread class or implements the Runnable interface.

2.  Override the run() method in your class. This method will contain the code to be executed by the thread.

3.  Create an instance of your class and call the start() method to begin the thread's execution.

Here's a simple Java example:

```java
class MyThread extends Thread {
    public void run() {
        for (int i = 0; i < 5; i++) {
            System.out.println("Thread 1: " + i);
        }
    }
}
```

143

```java
public class Main {
    public static void main(String[] args) {
        MyThread thread1 = new MyThread();
        thread1.start();

        for (int i = 0; i < 5; i++) {
            System.out.println("Main Thread: " + i);
        }
    }
}
```

In this example, we create a `MyThread` class that extends `Thread` and overrides the `run()` method. We then create an instance of this class and start it. The main thread and the custom thread run concurrently.

C++ Multithreading

C++ also supports multithreading through the Standard Library's `<thread>` header. To create a multithreaded application in C++, you can follow these steps:

1.   Include the `<thread>` header.

2.   Create a function or lambda that represents the code to be executed by the thread.

3.   Create a `std::thread` object and pass your function or lambda as an argument.

4.   Call the `join()` method on the thread object to wait for the thread to finish its execution.

Here's a simple C++ example:

```cpp
#include <iostream>
#include <thread>

void myFunction() {
    for (int i = 0; i < 5; i++) {
        std::cout << "Thread 1: " << i << std::endl;
    }
}

int main() {
    std::thread thread1(myFunction);

    for (int i = 0; i < 5; i++) {
        std::cout << "Main Thread: " << i << std::endl;
    }

    thread1.join();
```

```
    return 0;
}
```

In this C++ example, we define the `myFunction()` function, create a `std::thread` object called `thread1`, and join it to the main thread.

Both Java and C++ offer powerful features for multithreading, making them suitable choices for developing concurrent applications. However, managing thread synchronization and avoiding race conditions is crucial, which we will explore further in later sections.

---

## Section 13.3: Asynchronous Programming in JavaScript and Python

Asynchronous programming is essential for building responsive and efficient applications, especially in scenarios where tasks may take time to complete, such as network requests or file I/O. JavaScript and Python are two programming languages that excel in handling asynchronous operations through different mechanisms.

### Asynchronous Programming in JavaScript

In JavaScript, asynchronous programming is commonly achieved using callbacks, promises, and async/await.

1. **Callbacks:** Callbacks are functions passed as arguments to other functions. They are executed when an asynchronous operation completes. Callbacks can lead to callback hell or the "pyramid of doom" when dealing with multiple asynchronous operations.

   ```
   function fetchData(callback) {
       setTimeout(() => {
           const data = "Async data";
           callback(data);
       }, 1000);
   }

   fetchData((data) => {
       console.log(data);
   });
   ```

2. **Promises:** Promises provide a more structured way to handle asynchronous code. They represent a value that may be available now, in the future, or never. Promises allow chaining and error handling, making code more readable.

   ```
   function fetchData() {
       return new Promise((resolve, reject) => {
           setTimeout(() => {
               const data = "Async data";
               resolve(data);
   ```

```
        }, 1000);
    });
}

fetchData()
    .then((data) => {
        console.log(data);
    })
    .catch((error) => {
        console.error(error);
    });
```

3. **Async/Await:** Introduced in ECMAScript 2017, async/await is a syntactical improvement over promises. It makes asynchronous code appear more like synchronous code, enhancing readability.

```
async function fetchData() {
    return new Promise((resolve) => {
        setTimeout(() => {
            const data = "Async data";
            resolve(data);
        }, 1000);
    });
}

async function main() {
    try {
        const data = await fetchData();
        console.log(data);
    } catch (error) {
        console.error(error);
    }
}

main();
```

Asynchronous Programming in Python

Python also provides several mechanisms for asynchronous programming, including callbacks, threading, and the asyncio library for more advanced asynchronous operations.

1. **Callbacks:** Similar to JavaScript, Python can use callback functions to handle asynchronous tasks. Libraries like asyncio provide utilities for creating and managing callbacks.

```
import time

def fetch_data(callback):
    time.sleep(1)   # Simulate async operation
    data = "Async data"
```

```
        callback(data)

    def data_handler(data):
        print(data)

    fetch_data(data_handler)
```

2. **Threading:** Python supports threading for concurrent execution. Threads are suitable for I/O-bound tasks but may not utilize multiple CPU cores effectively due to the Global Interpreter Lock (GIL).

```
import threading

def print_numbers():
    for i in range(5):
        print("Thread 1:", i)

def print_letters():
    for letter in "ABCDE":
        print("Thread 2:", letter)

thread1 = threading.Thread(target=print_numbers)
thread2 = threading.Thread(target=print_letters)

thread1.start()
thread2.start()

thread1.join()
thread2.join()
```

3. **Asyncio:** The asyncio library in Python provides a powerful framework for asynchronous programming. It allows developers to write asynchronous code using async/await syntax and manage asynchronous I/O operations efficiently.

```
import asyncio

async def fetch_data():
    await asyncio.sleep(1)   # Simulate async operation
    return "Async data"

async def main():
    data = await fetch_data()
    print(data)

asyncio.run(main())
```

Both JavaScript and Python offer robust support for asynchronous programming, allowing developers to create responsive and efficient applications that handle concurrent tasks

147

effectively. The choice between these languages often depends on the specific requirements and use cases of the project.

---

## Section 13.4: Synchronization and Race Conditions

In concurrent programming, synchronization and race conditions are critical concepts to understand and manage. They deal with the coordination and interaction of multiple threads or processes accessing shared resources. Synchronization ensures that concurrent operations occur in a predictable order and avoid conflicts, while race conditions can lead to unexpected and erroneous behavior in multi-threaded or multi-process programs.

### Synchronization Mechanisms

To mitigate race conditions and ensure correct synchronization in concurrent programs, various synchronization mechanisms are used. Here are some common ones:

1. **Mutex (Mutual Exclusion):** Mutexes are used to protect critical sections of code from simultaneous execution by multiple threads. Only one thread can acquire a mutex at a time, ensuring exclusive access to a shared resource.

   ```python
   import threading

   mutex = threading.Lock()

   def critical_section():
       with mutex:
           # This code is protected by the mutex
           # Only one thread can execute it at a time
           pass
   ```

2. **Semaphore:** Semaphores are used to control access to a resource with a limited number of available slots. Threads can acquire and release semaphores to access the resource, ensuring that the resource is not overused.

   ```python
   import threading

   semaphore = threading.Semaphore(3)  # Allow 3 threads to access simulta
   neously

   def access_resource():
       with semaphore:
           # Up to 3 threads can execute this code concurrently
           pass
   ```

3.  **Condition Variable:** Condition variables allow threads to wait for a specific condition to be met before proceeding. They are often used for thread synchronization and signaling.

```python
import threading

condition = threading.Condition()

def wait_for_condition():
    with condition:
        while not some_condition:
            condition.wait()
            # Continue execution when the condition is met
```

## Race Conditions

Race conditions occur when multiple threads or processes access shared resources concurrently, and the final outcome depends on the relative timing of their execution. Race conditions can lead to unpredictable and incorrect results. Here's an example in Python:

```python
import threading

counter = 0

def increment_counter():
    global counter
    for _ in range(1000000):
        counter += 1

# Create two threads to increment the counter
thread1 = threading.Thread(target=increment_counter)
thread2 = threading.Thread(target=increment_counter)

thread1.start()
thread2.start()

thread1.join()
thread2.join()

print("Counter:", counter)  # The result may be unpredictable due to the race
condition
```

In this example, both threads increment the counter variable concurrently, leading to a race condition. The final value of counter is unpredictable and may not be the expected 2000000.

To address race conditions, synchronization mechanisms like mutexes or semaphores can be used to ensure that only one thread accesses the shared resource at a time. This prevents data corruption and ensures the program's correctness.

Understanding synchronization mechanisms and being mindful of race conditions are essential for developing robust concurrent applications that behave as expected and avoid unexpected issues.

---

## Section 13.5: Real-World Applications of Concurrent Programming

Concurrent programming plays a crucial role in modern software development, enabling applications to efficiently utilize multi-core processors and handle multiple tasks simultaneously. In this section, we will explore real-world applications and scenarios where concurrent programming is essential.

### 1. Web Servers

Web servers need to handle multiple incoming requests concurrently, ensuring efficient processing and quick response times. Each incoming request is typically processed in a separate thread or process, allowing the server to handle numerous clients simultaneously. Technologies like Node.js, Django, and Apache use concurrent programming to achieve this.

### 2. Video Game Engines

Video game engines require complex simulations and rendering processes. Concurrent programming is used to manage tasks like physics simulations, AI behavior, and rendering. Multithreading and parallelism help in distributing these tasks across CPU cores for optimal performance.

### 3. Database Systems

Database systems often need to manage multiple client connections and execute queries concurrently. Concurrency control mechanisms, like locking, help ensure data consistency and integrity in multi-user database environments.

### 4. Operating Systems

Operating systems themselves are concurrent entities. They manage processes, threads, and hardware resources concurrently to provide a responsive and efficient environment for running applications. The scheduler, file system, and device drivers are examples of components that rely on concurrency.

### 5. Parallel Computing

High-performance computing (HPC) applications, scientific simulations, and data processing tasks benefit greatly from parallelism and concurrent programming. Technologies like OpenMP and MPI enable developers to create parallel applications that utilize the full power of supercomputers and clusters.

## 6. Networking

Networking applications, such as peer-to-peer file sharing, online gaming, and real-time communication, require efficient handling of data streams from multiple sources. Concurrent programming helps manage network connections and data transmission efficiently.

## 7. Financial Systems

Financial systems process vast amounts of data, such as stock market trades and transactions. Concurrent programming ensures timely and accurate processing of financial data, allowing for real-time analytics and decision-making.

## 8. IoT (Internet of Things)

IoT devices often generate and transmit data concurrently. Cloud-based IoT platforms use concurrent programming to handle data ingestion, processing, and storage from numerous devices in real time.

## 9. Video Streaming

Video streaming services need to transmit video and audio data to multiple viewers simultaneously. Concurrent programming optimizes the distribution of data and ensures a smooth streaming experience.

## 10. Search Engines

Search engines like Google index and retrieve web pages from the internet in parallel. Concurrent processing of search queries and distributed systems help provide fast and relevant search results.

In conclusion, concurrent programming is an indispensable aspect of modern software development. It enables applications to efficiently utilize hardware resources, respond to user demands in real time, and handle large-scale data processing. Understanding the principles of concurrent programming and choosing the right concurrency mechanisms are essential for building robust and scalable software systems in various domains.

---

# Chapter 14: Libraries, Frameworks, and APIs

## Section 14.1: The Role of Libraries in Software Development

Libraries, frameworks, and APIs (Application Programming Interfaces) are fundamental components of modern software development. They play a pivotal role in simplifying and accelerating the software development process. In this section, we'll focus on the importance of libraries and how they contribute to building robust and efficient software.

Libraries are collections of pre-written code, functions, and routines that developers can use to perform common tasks without reinventing the wheel. They encapsulate specific functionalities, making them accessible through a well-defined interface. Here are some key points regarding the significance of libraries in software development:

1. **Code Reusability**: Libraries promote code reusability. Developers can leverage existing libraries to solve common problems, saving time and effort. This reusability reduces redundancy in codebases and leads to more maintainable software.

2. **Accelerated Development**: Libraries provide a shortcut to implementing complex features. Instead of writing code from scratch, developers can integrate libraries that have already solved similar challenges. This speeds up development cycles and allows for faster time-to-market.

3. **Reliability**: Established libraries have been tested and used by a wide developer community. This collective experience enhances the reliability of the code. Bugs and issues are often discovered and fixed quickly, reducing the risk of critical failures.

4. **Performance Optimization**: Libraries are often optimized for performance. They are written by experts who focus on efficiency and correctness. Utilizing well-optimized libraries can significantly enhance the performance of an application.

5. **Cross-Platform Compatibility**: Many libraries are designed to be cross-platform, meaning they can be used on various operating systems and platforms. This simplifies the development process for applications targeting multiple environments.

6. **Ecosystem Support**: Libraries are usually part of larger ecosystems. For example, JavaScript libraries are widely used in web development, and Python has a rich ecosystem of libraries for data science and machine learning. Developers can benefit from a supportive community and a wealth of resources.

7. **Specialized Functionality**: Libraries often focus on specific domains or functionalities. For instance, there are libraries for graphics rendering, networking, cryptography, and more. This specialization allows developers to leverage domain-specific expertise.

8. **Interoperability**: Libraries enable interoperability between different software components. They provide standardized interfaces that applications can use to communicate with each other, regardless of the underlying technologies.

9. **Reduced Complexity**: Libraries abstract complex operations into simple function calls. This abstraction reduces the cognitive load on developers, allowing them to focus on higher-level application logic rather than low-level details.

10. **Community Contributions**: Open-source libraries benefit from contributions from a global developer community. This collaborative approach ensures that libraries stay up-to-date, secure, and adaptable to evolving requirements.

In summary, libraries are indispensable tools in software development. They empower developers to build feature-rich, reliable, and performant applications while reducing development time and effort. As technology continues to evolve, libraries will remain a cornerstone of efficient and effective software engineering.

---

## Section 14.2: Popular Frameworks for Web Development

Web development has evolved significantly over the years, and one of the key reasons behind this evolution is the availability of powerful frameworks. These frameworks provide developers with the tools, structure, and best practices needed to build sophisticated web applications efficiently. In this section, we'll explore some of the popular frameworks used in web development.

1. **Angular**: Developed and maintained by Google, Angular is a robust JavaScript framework for building dynamic, single-page web applications. It offers features like two-way data binding, dependency injection, and a comprehensive set of tools for routing, form handling, and testing. Angular simplifies the development of complex web applications by promoting modularity and maintainability.

2. **React**: Created by Facebook, React is a JavaScript library for building user interfaces. While not a full-fledged framework, React is widely used in combination with other libraries and tools to create interactive and reusable UI components. Its virtual DOM and component-based architecture make it highly efficient for building modern web applications.

3. **Vue.js**: Vue.js is a progressive JavaScript framework that focuses on the view layer of web applications. It is known for its simplicity and ease of integration into existing projects. Vue.js allows developers to incrementally adopt its features, making it a great choice for both small and large-scale applications.

4. **Ruby on Rails**: Often referred to as Rails, Ruby on Rails is a web application framework written in Ruby. It follows the convention over configuration (CoC) and don't repeat yourself (DRY) principles, which emphasize simplicity and productivity. Rails provides a robust set of tools for building database-backed web applications.

5. **Django**: Django is a high-level Python web framework that prioritizes rapid development and clean, pragmatic design. It includes an ORM (Object-Relational Mapping) system, authentication, and an admin interface out of the box, simplifying the development of database-driven web applications.

6. **Express.js**: Express.js is a minimal and flexible Node.js web application framework that provides a robust set of features for web and mobile applications. It is

commonly used for building APIs and server-side applications. Express.js is known for its simplicity and speed.

7. **Laravel**: Laravel is a popular PHP framework known for its elegant syntax and developer-friendly features. It simplifies tasks such as routing, authentication, caching, and database management, allowing developers to focus on building feature-rich web applications.

8. **Spring Boot**: Spring Boot is an extension of the Spring framework for building Java-based web applications. It aims to simplify the development process by providing production-ready defaults for setting up Spring applications. Spring Boot is well-suited for building enterprise-grade applications.

9. **Flask**: Flask is a lightweight Python web framework that is often described as a micro-framework due to its simplicity and minimalism. It is highly extensible and suitable for small to medium-sized web applications and APIs.

10. **ASP.NET Core**: Developed by Microsoft, ASP.NET Core is a cross-platform framework for building modern, cloud-based, and internet-connected applications. It supports multiple programming languages and includes features for building web APIs and web applications.

These are just a few examples of the many frameworks available for web development. The choice of framework often depends on factors like programming language preference, project requirements, scalability, and the development team's familiarity with the framework. Regardless of the choice, frameworks play a crucial role in streamlining the development process and ensuring the creation of robust web applications.

---

## Section 14.3: API Integration and Management

In modern web development, applications often rely on external services and data sources to enhance their functionality. This integration is made possible through Application Programming Interfaces (APIs), which allow different software systems to communicate with each other. In this section, we will explore the importance of API integration and how it is managed in web development.

### The Significance of API Integration

APIs are like bridges that connect different software components, services, and platforms. They enable developers to leverage existing functionality and data in their applications, reducing the need to reinvent the wheel. Here are some key reasons why API integration is significant:

1. **Access to External Services**: APIs provide access to a wide range of external services, such as social media platforms, payment gateways, mapping services, and

more. This access allows developers to enrich their applications with features that would be time-consuming or impractical to build from scratch.

2. **Data Enrichment**: APIs allow applications to fetch real-time data from external sources. For example, weather applications can use APIs to provide current weather conditions and forecasts based on data from meteorological services.

3. **Improved User Experience**: Integrating APIs can enhance the user experience by providing additional features and functionalities. For instance, an e-commerce website can integrate a payment gateway API to facilitate secure online transactions.

4. **Scalability**: API integration enables applications to scale efficiently by offloading certain tasks to specialized services. This scalability is essential for handling increased user traffic and data processing demands.

API Management

While API integration offers numerous benefits, it also comes with challenges related to security, scalability, and maintenance. API management plays a crucial role in addressing these challenges:

1. **Security**: APIs can expose sensitive data and functionality. Proper authentication and authorization mechanisms are essential to secure API endpoints and ensure that only authorized users or applications can access them.

2. **Rate Limiting**: To prevent abuse or overuse of APIs, rate limiting can be applied. This restricts the number of requests a client can make within a specific time frame, ensuring fair usage and resource availability.

3. **Documentation**: Clear and comprehensive API documentation is essential for developers who want to integrate an API. It should provide details on available endpoints, request parameters, response formats, and usage examples.

4. **Monitoring and Analytics**: API management tools often include monitoring and analytics features. These tools track API usage, identify performance bottlenecks, and provide insights into how APIs are being utilized.

5. **Versioning**: As APIs evolve, it's essential to maintain backward compatibility to avoid breaking existing integrations. Versioning allows developers to specify which version of an API they want to use.

Popular API Management Tools

Several API management tools and platforms are available to streamline the process of integrating and managing APIs. Some popular options include:

- **Apigee**: Google's Apigee offers a comprehensive API management platform with features for security, analytics, and developer collaboration.

- **AWS API Gateway**: Amazon Web Services provides a managed API Gateway service that makes it easy to create, publish, and monitor APIs.

- **Azure API Management**: Microsoft's Azure API Management offers a platform for building, deploying, and scaling APIs.

- **Postman**: While primarily known as a popular API testing tool, Postman also offers API collaboration and monitoring features.

- **Swagger (OpenAPI)**: Swagger is an open-source framework for designing, building, and documenting RESTful APIs. It provides a standardized way to describe APIs.

In conclusion, API integration is a fundamental aspect of modern web development, enabling applications to access external services and data. Effective API management is crucial for maintaining security, scalability, and developer-friendly experiences. As web applications continue to rely on external APIs, the role of API integration and management will only become more vital in the software development landscape.

---

## Section 14.4: Cross-Language Compatibility and Bridging

In the diverse landscape of programming languages, it's common to encounter scenarios where different languages need to interact and collaborate within the same software project. This can happen for various reasons, such as leveraging existing libraries, using languages with different strengths, or integrating legacy code. In this section, we'll explore the challenges and techniques involved in achieving cross-language compatibility and bridging.

### Why Cross-Language Compatibility Matters

Cross-language compatibility is essential for several reasons:

1. **Leveraging Existing Code**: Organizations may have invested heavily in codebases written in different languages. Reusing this code can save time and resources.

2. **Specialization**: Some languages excel in specific domains. For example, C and C++ are known for their performance, while Python is valued for its simplicity. Combining these languages allows developers to take advantage of their strengths.

3. **Legacy Systems**: Legacy systems are often written in languages that are no longer in widespread use. Bridging these systems with modern languages can extend their lifespan and functionality.

4. **Interoperability**: Different languages might be chosen for different components of a project. For instance, a web application may use JavaScript for the frontend and Python for backend server logic.

## Techniques for Cross-Language Compatibility

Achieving cross-language compatibility typically involves the following techniques:

### 1. Foreign Function Interfaces (FFI)

FFI is a mechanism that allows code written in one language to call functions implemented in another language. It provides a standardized way to interface with native code. Many languages offer FFI libraries or extensions for this purpose. For example, Python has the `ctypes` library for calling C functions, and Java has Java Native Interface (JNI) for interacting with native code.

### 2. Language Bindings

Language bindings provide a higher-level API for interacting with a library or framework written in another language. These bindings are typically generated automatically based on the target language's conventions. For instance, there are Python bindings for libraries written in C or C++ that provide a Pythonic interface to those libraries, making it easier for Python developers to use them.

### 3. Web APIs

When dealing with web applications, using web APIs can be an effective way to achieve cross-language compatibility. RESTful APIs, for example, allow different languages to communicate over HTTP by sending and receiving data in standardized formats like JSON or XML. This approach is language-agnostic and commonly used in microservices architectures.

### 4. Message Queues and Protocols

Message queuing systems like RabbitMQ and protocols like MQTT enable communication between components written in different languages. These systems allow messages to be exchanged asynchronously, facilitating decoupled and distributed architectures.

### 5. Standard Data Formats

Using standard data formats like JSON, XML, Protocol Buffers, or Apache Avro can enable different languages to exchange data seamlessly. Libraries for parsing and generating these formats are available for most programming languages.

## Challenges in Cross-Language Compatibility

While cross-language compatibility is valuable, it comes with challenges:

1. **Data Type Mismatch**: Different languages may represent data types differently. Mapping data types between languages can be error-prone.

2. **Memory Management**: Languages may have different memory management models (e.g., manual memory management in C/C++ and automatic memory management in Python). Care must be taken when passing data between them.

3.  **Error Handling**: Handling errors and exceptions across language boundaries can be complex, as each language may have its error handling mechanisms.

4.  **Performance Overhead**: Interfacing between languages can introduce performance overhead, especially in situations where data needs to be converted or copied.

5.  **Debugging and Testing**: Debugging and testing code that spans multiple languages can be challenging, as debugging tools may not seamlessly support all languages involved.

In conclusion, achieving cross-language compatibility and bridging is crucial when building complex software systems that involve different languages. It enables developers to make the most of each language's strengths and reuse existing code. However, it also comes with challenges related to data types, memory management, error handling, performance, debugging, and testing. Careful planning and consideration of these challenges are essential for successful cross-language integration in software development projects.

---

## Section 14.5: Evaluating and Choosing the Right Tools

Selecting the appropriate libraries, frameworks, and APIs for your software project is a critical decision that can significantly impact its success. In this section, we'll discuss the process of evaluating and choosing the right tools for the job.

### The Importance of Tool Selection

Choosing the right tools is essential for several reasons:

1.  **Efficiency**: The right tools can help developers work more efficiently, reducing development time and costs.

2.  **Functionality**: Different tools offer varying levels of functionality. Selecting tools that align with your project's requirements is crucial.

3.  **Compatibility**: Tools should be compatible with your existing technology stack. Incompatible tools can lead to integration issues and inefficiencies.

4.  **Scalability**: Tools should be capable of scaling with your project's growth. Scalability ensures that your software can handle increased user loads and data.

5.  **Community and Support**: Tools with active communities and robust support systems are more likely to receive updates, bug fixes, and security patches.

### Evaluating Tools

When evaluating tools, consider the following factors:

## 1. Project Requirements

Start by understanding your project's requirements. What functionality does your software need? What technologies are you already using? Your tool selection should align with these requirements.

## 2. User Experience

Consider the user experience your tool provides. Is it easy to use? Does it have a user-friendly interface? A tool that simplifies tasks for developers can boost productivity.

## 3. Documentation

Check the quality and comprehensiveness of the tool's documentation. Good documentation can save developers time and help them troubleshoot issues.

## 4. Community and Support

Evaluate the tool's community and support. Are there active forums or mailing lists where developers can seek help? Are there regular updates and bug fixes?

## 5. Licensing and Costs

Understand the licensing and costs associated with the tool. Some tools may be open source, while others require a licensing fee. Consider your budget and licensing constraints.

## 6. Performance

Performance is critical. Tools should not introduce significant performance overhead. Test the tool's impact on your software's performance before adoption.

## 7. Integration

Ensure that the tool integrates smoothly with your existing technology stack. Integration difficulties can lead to delays and compatibility issues.

## 8. Security

Security is paramount. Assess the tool's security features and track record. Using insecure tools can lead to vulnerabilities in your software.

## 9. Vendor Lock-In

Be cautious of tools that create vendor lock-in, making it challenging to switch to alternatives. Favor tools that offer flexibility and interoperability.

## 10. Scalability

Consider the tool's scalability. Can it handle your project's growth? Scalability ensures your software remains responsive as user loads increase.

After evaluating tools based on these factors, create a shortlist of options that best meet your project's requirements. Consider conducting proof-of-concept or pilot projects to assess how well the tools perform in your specific context.

Finally, involve your development team in the decision-making process. Developers who will be using the tools have valuable insights into their practicality and effectiveness.

Remember that tool selection is not a one-time decision. As your project evolves, periodically reassess your toolset to ensure it continues to meet your needs. Making informed choices about the tools you use is crucial for the success of your software development projects.

# Chapter 15: Debugging and Testing

Debugging and testing are essential aspects of the software development process. In this chapter, we'll delve into the principles and practices of effective debugging and testing techniques.

## Section 15.1: Principles of Effective Debugging

Debugging is the process of identifying and fixing errors or bugs in your software. Effective debugging not only helps in resolving issues but also enhances your overall programming skills. Here are some fundamental principles of effective debugging:

### 1. Reproduce the Issue

Before you can fix a bug, you need to reproduce it consistently. Understand the conditions and steps that lead to the problem's occurrence. Without a reliable way to trigger the issue, debugging becomes challenging.

### 2. Understand the Code

Thoroughly understand the code related to the problem. This includes not only the code where the bug manifests but also any relevant dependencies. The more you understand the code, the easier it is to pinpoint issues.

### 3. Use Version Control

Version control systems like Git are invaluable for tracking changes in your codebase. Commits can serve as checkpoints, allowing you to revert to a working state if necessary. Use meaningful commit messages to document changes.

### 4. Start with Assertions

Incorporate assertions into your code to catch issues early. Assertions are statements that check whether certain conditions hold true. If an assertion fails, it indicates a problem. Assertions can help you detect issues closer to their source.

### 5. Divide and Conquer

Divide complex problems into smaller, manageable parts. Debug each part individually to identify the root cause. This approach is particularly helpful when dealing with large codebases.

### 6. Use Debugging Tools

Modern integrated development environments (IDEs) provide powerful debugging tools. Learn how to use breakpoints, watch variables, and step through code. These tools allow you to inspect program state at different points in execution.

### 7. Replicate the Environment

Consider the environment in which the bug occurs. Differences in operating systems, hardware, or external factors can influence behavior. If possible, replicate the environment to test and debug effectively.

### 8. Keep a Log

Logging is a valuable debugging technique. Insert log statements at strategic points in your code to track its execution. Logs can provide insights into the program's flow and identify unexpected behavior.

### 9. Collaborate and Seek Help

Don't hesitate to seek help from colleagues or online developer communities. Explaining the issue to someone else can often lead to insights. Collaborative debugging can be more efficient.

### 10. Test Your Fixes

Once you identify and fix a bug, test the solution rigorously. Verify that the issue is resolved and that the fix doesn't introduce new problems. Automated testing can help ensure consistent behavior.

### 11. Document the Solution

Document the bug's details, the steps to reproduce it, and the solution. Good documentation helps not only your future self but also other team members who may encounter similar issues.

Debugging is a skill that improves with practice. Embrace challenges as opportunities to enhance your problem-solving abilities. Remember that every bug you encounter is a chance to become a better programmer.

In the following sections of this chapter, we'll explore different testing methodologies, tools, and best practices to complement your debugging skills.

---

## Section 15.2: Unit Testing and Test-Driven Development

Unit testing is a fundamental practice in software development that focuses on testing individual components, or units, of your code in isolation. Test-Driven Development (TDD) is an approach that emphasizes writing tests before writing the actual code. In this section, we'll explore these concepts in more detail.

## What is Unit Testing?

Unit testing involves breaking your code into small, testable units. These units are typically functions, methods, or classes that perform specific tasks. The goal of unit testing is to verify that each unit of code behaves as expected when given certain inputs.

Unit tests are automated and can be run frequently, ensuring that changes to your codebase do not introduce regressions. They provide a safety net that helps catch and fix issues early in the development process.

## Benefits of Unit Testing

1. **Early Detection of Bugs:** Unit tests can catch bugs as soon as they are introduced, making it easier and cheaper to fix them.

2. **Improved Code Quality:** Writing tests forces you to think about your code's design and interface, leading to more modular and maintainable code.

3. **Documentation:** Unit tests serve as documentation for how your code is expected to behave. This is especially helpful for other developers who work on the codebase.

4. **Regression Prevention:** As your codebase grows, unit tests help ensure that existing functionality continues to work as expected when new features are added.

## Test-Driven Development (TDD)

TDD is a development methodology that revolves around writing tests before writing the actual code. The TDD cycle typically consists of three steps:

1. **Write a Test:** Start by writing a unit test that specifies the behavior you want to implement. This test will initially fail because the code it tests does not exist yet.

2. **Write the Code:** Implement the minimum amount of code necessary to make the test pass. This often involves creating new functions or modifying existing ones.

3. **Refactor:** Once the test passes, you can refactor the code to improve its design or performance while keeping the tests green (passing). This step ensures that you maintain code quality as you add new features.

## Example of TDD

Let's consider a simple example using Python and the built-in unittest library. Suppose you want to create a function that adds two numbers. Here's how you might follow the TDD process:

1. **Write a Test (test_addition.py):**

```
import unittest
from my_math import add

class TestAddition(unittest.TestCase):
```

```
def test_add_positive_numbers(self):
    result = add(2, 3)
    self.assertEqual(result, 5)

def test_add_negative_numbers(self):
    result = add(-2, -3)
    self.assertEqual(result, -5)
```

2. **Write the Code (my_math.py):**

```
def add(a, b):
    return a + b
```

3. **Run the Tests:**

   Run the tests using a test runner (e.g., `unittest` or a testing framework like `pytest`). If all tests pass, you can be confident in the correctness of your code.

Unit testing and TDD are valuable practices that help ensure code quality, reduce bugs, and make your codebase more maintainable. Incorporating these practices into your development workflow can lead to more robust software.

---

## Section 15.3: Debugging Tools and Techniques for Each Language

Debugging is a critical skill for developers, as it allows them to identify and fix issues in their code. Different programming languages come with various debugging tools and techniques. In this section, we'll explore debugging tools and best practices for some popular programming languages.

### Python

Python offers a range of debugging tools and techniques:

1. **print() Statements:** The simplest way to debug Python code is by adding print statements to your code to output variable values or messages at specific points in your program. While straightforward, it can be effective for debugging.

2. **pdb Debugger:** Python's built-in debugger, pdb, allows you to set breakpoints, step through code, and inspect variables interactively. You can start the debugger by importing pdb and adding `pdb.set_trace()` at the desired location in your code.

3. **IDEs with Debugging Support:** Integrated Development Environments (IDEs) like PyCharm, Visual Studio Code, and PyDev offer powerful debugging features, including breakpoints, variable inspection, and stepping through code.

## Java

Java developers have access to several debugging tools and techniques:

1.  **System.out.println():** Similar to Python's print statements, Java developers often use `System.out.println()` to print messages and variable values to the console for debugging purposes.

2.  **IDE Debugging:** Java IDEs like Eclipse, IntelliJ IDEA, and NetBeans provide sophisticated debugging capabilities. Developers can set breakpoints, step through code, and inspect variables.

3.  **jdb Debugger:** Java also includes a command-line debugger called `jdb`, which allows developers to debug their code interactively. It's useful when working outside of an IDE.

## C and C++

Debugging C and C++ code often involves the following techniques:

1.  **printf Statements:** Developers frequently use `printf` statements to print debug information to the console. This technique is straightforward and effective for understanding program flow.

2.  **GDB Debugger:** The GNU Debugger (GDB) is a powerful command-line debugger for C and C++. It offers features like breakpoints, stepping through code, and examining variables. GDB can be used in combination with an IDE or as a standalone tool.

3.  **IDE Debugging:** IDEs like Visual Studio, CLion, and Code::Blocks provide integrated debugging tools with features like breakpoints, variable inspection, and memory analysis.

## JavaScript

JavaScript debugging can be achieved through various methods:

1.  **console.log():** Similar to print statements in other languages, developers often use `console.log()` to output information to the browser's console. This method is widely used for debugging JavaScript in web applications.

2.  **Browser Developer Tools:** Modern web browsers come with built-in developer tools that include a JavaScript debugger. Developers can set breakpoints, step through code, and inspect variables directly within the browser.

3.  **Node.js Debugging:** For server-side JavaScript (Node.js), you can use the `--inspect` or `--inspect-brk` flags to enable debugging. Tools like Chrome DevTools can be used to attach to a Node.js process for debugging.

Regardless of the programming language, here are some best practices for effective debugging:

1. **Start Small:** When encountering an issue, try to isolate it by reducing the code to the smallest possible example that still reproduces the problem.

2. **Use Version Control:** Keep your codebase under version control (e.g., Git) so that you can easily revert to a working state if needed.

3. **Document Issues:** Create clear and detailed bug reports or comments when you identify issues. This documentation can be helpful when working in a team.

4. **Learn the Tools:** Invest time in learning the debugging tools and techniques specific to your chosen language and development environment.

5. **Practice and Patience:** Debugging is a skill that improves with practice. Be patient, and don't hesitate to seek help from online communities or colleagues when you're stuck.

Effective debugging is a crucial skill for developers, and mastering the tools and techniques available for your programming language can significantly improve your productivity and code quality.

## Section 15.4: Integration and System Testing

Integration and system testing are essential phases in the software development life cycle. They help ensure that individual components or modules of a software system work together seamlessly and that the entire system functions as intended. In this section, we will discuss the concepts of integration testing and system testing, their objectives, techniques, and best practices.

### Integration Testing

Integration testing focuses on verifying the interactions and interfaces between different software components or modules. Its primary objectives are:

1. **Detecting Interface Issues:** Integration testing identifies problems that may arise when different modules or components communicate. These issues include data flow problems, parameter mismatches, and incorrect function calls.

2. **Assessing Data Flow:** It ensures that data flows correctly between integrated components. This includes testing data transformation, validation, and transmission between modules.

3. **Functional Validations:** Integration tests also verify that the combined functionality of integrated components meets the specified requirements.

There are several integration testing strategies:

- **Top-Down Testing:** In this approach, testing begins with the main module and progressively incorporates lower-level modules. Stubs (simplified versions of lower-level modules) may be used to simulate their behavior.

- **Bottom-Up Testing:** Here, the testing starts with lower-level modules, and higher-level modules are added incrementally. Drivers (simplified versions of higher-level modules) simulate their behavior.

- **Big Bang Testing:** All components are integrated simultaneously, and the entire system is tested. This approach may be suitable for small projects but can be challenging for larger systems.

## System Testing

System testing evaluates the complete software system as a whole. It aims to ensure that the integrated components function together harmoniously and meet the specified requirements. The key objectives of system testing are:

1. **Validating System Behavior:** System tests validate that the software system behaves correctly, adhering to functional and non-functional requirements.

2. **Performance and Scalability Testing:** It assesses system performance under various conditions, including load testing, stress testing, and scalability testing.

3. **Security Testing:** Security-related tests check for vulnerabilities, such as data breaches, unauthorized access, and authentication issues.

4. **Usability and User Acceptance:** User experience and acceptance tests ensure that the system is user-friendly and meets user expectations.

System testing includes various types of tests:

- **Functional Testing:** Verifies that the software functions correctly according to the specified requirements.

- **Performance Testing:** Assesses system performance under different loads to identify bottlenecks and optimize performance.

- **Security Testing:** Focuses on identifying vulnerabilities and ensuring data protection.

- **Usability Testing:** Evaluates the user interface, ease of navigation, and user satisfaction.

- **Compatibility Testing:** Ensures the software functions correctly on different platforms, browsers, or devices.

- **Regression Testing:** Validates that new changes or features have not introduced regressions in existing functionality.

### Best Practices for Integration and System Testing

Effective integration and system testing require careful planning and execution. Here are some best practices to follow:

1. **Define Clear Test Objectives:** Clearly define what each test aims to achieve, including the expected outcomes.

2. **Use Realistic Test Data:** Ensure that test data closely resembles real-world scenarios to validate system behavior accurately.

3. **Automate Testing:** Automate repetitive and complex test scenarios to improve efficiency and repeatability.

4. **Execute Comprehensive Test Cases:** Cover a wide range of scenarios, including edge cases and error conditions.

5. **Monitor and Document Results:** Continuously monitor test execution and document test results and any issues encountered.

6. **Prioritize Security:** Include security testing throughout the development process to identify vulnerabilities early.

7. **Involve Stakeholders:** Include end-users or stakeholders in acceptance testing to validate that the system meets their expectations.

8. **Perform Regular Regression Testing:** Ensure that new changes do not break existing functionality by conducting regression tests.

Integration and system testing are critical stages in the software development process, helping to ensure that a software system functions correctly, performs well, and meets user expectations. Properly planned and executed testing can significantly reduce the risk of post-release issues and enhance the overall quality of the software.

---

### Section 15.5: Building a Robust Testing Framework

Building a robust testing framework is a fundamental aspect of software development. A well-structured testing framework streamlines the testing process, enhances test coverage, and ensures that the software meets quality standards. In this section, we will discuss the key considerations and best practices for creating an effective testing framework.

1. **Test Strategy:** Begin by defining a clear testing strategy. Decide what types of testing (unit, integration, system, etc.) are required for your project, and how they will be implemented.

2. **Test Automation:** Whenever possible, automate your tests. Automated tests are repeatable, efficient, and provide fast feedback. Tools like JUnit, Selenium, and PyTest are popular choices for test automation.

3. **Test Data:** Ensure that your testing framework includes mechanisms for managing test data. Having a consistent and reliable dataset is crucial for testing various scenarios.

4. **Test Reporting:** Implement a robust reporting mechanism that provides detailed information about test execution, including passed and failed tests, coverage metrics, and performance data.

5. **Test Environment:** Maintain separate testing environments that closely mimic the production environment. This helps in testing real-world scenarios without affecting live systems.

6. **Continuous Integration:** Integrate your testing framework with a continuous integration (CI) system such as Jenkins, Travis CI, or CircleCI. This ensures that tests are automatically executed whenever code changes are pushed, providing early feedback to developers.

7. **Test Coverage:** Aim for high test coverage by ensuring that your tests exercise various code paths. Tools like JaCoCo (Java), coverage.py (Python), and Istanbul (JavaScript) can help measure code coverage.

Best Practices for Building a Testing Framework

Here are some best practices to consider when building a testing framework:

1. **Modularity:** Design your testing framework to be modular, allowing you to add, remove, or modify tests and test cases easily.

2. **Reusability:** Create reusable test components, such as utility functions and fixtures, to avoid duplication of code.

3. **Test Data Management:** Implement mechanisms for managing test data, including data generation, seeding, and cleanup. Using a test database or mock data can be beneficial.

4. **Test Suites:** Organize tests into suites based on functionality or modules. This makes it easier to run specific groups of tests.

5. **Parameterized Tests:** Use parameterized tests to run the same test with multiple sets of input data, reducing code duplication.

6. **Parallel Execution:** If your testing framework supports it, run tests in parallel to save time and resources.

7. **Failure Handling:** Implement mechanisms to handle test failures gracefully, including capturing screenshots or logs for further analysis.

8. **Continuous Maintenance:** Regularly update and maintain your testing framework to keep it compatible with the evolving codebase and changing requirements.

9. **Documentation:** Document your testing framework, including how to write and execute tests, so that team members can use it effectively.

10. **Integration with CI/CD:** Ensure seamless integration with your CI/CD pipeline, enabling automated testing with each code commit and deployment.

Example Testing Framework (Python with PyTest)

Here's a simplified example of a testing framework using Python and PyTest:

```python
# File: test_calculator.py

import pytest
from calculator import add, subtract, multiply, divide

@pytest.mark.parametrize("a, b, expected", [
    (2, 3, 5),
    (10, 5, 5),
    (0, 0, 0),
])
def test_addition(a, b, expected):
    result = add(a, b)
    assert result == expected

def test_subtraction():
    result = subtract(10, 5)
    assert result == 5

def test_multiplication():
    result = multiply(2, 3)
    assert result == 6

def test_division():
    result = divide(10, 2)
    assert result == 5
```

In this example, we have a simple testing framework for a calculator application. We use PyTest's parameterization feature to run the same addition test with different input values. This demonstrates how a testing framework can simplify and automate the testing process.

Remember that the complexity of your testing framework should match the needs of your project. For larger projects, you may need more sophisticated setups, including test data management, mocking, and advanced reporting. Building a robust testing framework is an investment that pays off by ensuring software quality and reliability.

# Chapter 16: Version Control and Collaboration

## Section 16.1: Introduction to Version Control Systems

Version control systems (VCS) are essential tools for software development, enabling teams to efficiently manage code, track changes, collaborate seamlessly, and maintain a history of their project's evolution. In this section, we'll delve into the fundamental concepts of version control systems and explore their significance in modern software development.

### What Is Version Control?

At its core, version control is a system that records changes made to files over time. It allows developers to:

1. **Track Changes:** Version control systems keep a detailed record of every modification made to a project, including who made the change, when it was made, and the nature of the change.

2. **Collaborate Effectively:** Multiple team members can work on the same codebase simultaneously. Version control systems ensure that changes don't conflict and can be merged smoothly.

3. **Revert to Previous States:** If an issue arises or a mistake is made, developers can easily roll back to a previous version of the code, minimizing the risk of data loss.

4. **Maintain a History:** VCS maintains a chronological history of changes, allowing developers to review past versions, understand why certain decisions were made, and trace the evolution of the project.

### Types of Version Control Systems

There are two main categories of version control systems:

1. **Centralized VCS:** In a centralized VCS, there is a single, central repository that holds the entire history of the project. Developers check out code from this central location, make changes, and commit them back to the central repository. Examples include CVS (Concurrent Versions System) and SVN (Apache Subversion).

2. **Distributed VCS:** Distributed VCS, also known as DVCS, offers a more decentralized approach. Each developer maintains a local copy of the repository, including the full history. They can work independently and synchronize their changes with others' repositories. Git and Mercurial are popular distributed VCSs.

### Advantages of Version Control Systems

Version control systems offer numerous advantages:

- **Collaboration:** Team members can work together on the same project without stepping on each other's toes.

- **History Tracking:** Detailed logs of changes help in diagnosing issues, understanding code evolution, and auditing.

- **Branching and Merging:** Developers can create branches to work on new features or bug fixes independently. Merging branches back into the main codebase is typically straightforward.

- **Code Review:** VCS facilitates code review processes, ensuring that changes are thoroughly examined before integration.

- **Backup and Recovery:** Data loss is mitigated as the entire project history is stored in the VCS.

In the next sections, we will explore specific version control systems, focusing on Git, one of the most widely used distributed version control systems in the software development industry. We will delve into its features, best practices, and how to set up and use Git effectively in collaborative coding environments.

Stay tuned to unlock the power of version control and elevate your software development workflow.

---

## Section 16.2: Collaborative Coding with Git

Git is a powerful and widely adopted distributed version control system (DVCS) that revolutionized how developers collaborate on software projects. In this section, we'll delve into Git's core concepts and explore how it enables seamless collaborative coding.

### Understanding Git Basics

Git operates on the principles of distributed version control, which means that each developer has a complete copy of the project's repository, including its entire history. Here are some fundamental Git concepts:

1. **Repository (Repo):** A Git repository is a folder containing all project files and their complete history. It's the central place where changes are tracked.

2. **Commit:** A commit is a snapshot of the project at a specific point in time. It records changes made to the files, along with a message describing the changes' purpose.

3. **Branch:** A branch is a separate line of development. It allows developers to work on new features or bug fixes without affecting the main codebase. Branches can be created, switched, and merged.

4. **Remote:** A remote is a copy of a Git repository stored on a different server. Developers can push (upload) their changes to a remote and pull (download) changes from it. Common remote hosting services include GitHub, GitLab, and Bitbucket.

5. **Pull Request (PR):** In Git-based collaboration, a pull request is a proposed code change that one developer wants to merge into another branch. It serves as a request for others to review and approve the changes.

## Collaborative Workflows

Git facilitates various collaborative workflows, enabling teams to work together efficiently. Here are a few common Git workflows:

1. **Feature Branch Workflow:** Developers create feature branches to work on specific features or bug fixes. When ready, they submit pull requests to merge their changes into the main branch.

2. **Gitflow Workflow:** This structured workflow defines specific branches for features, releases, and hotfixes. It's suitable for projects with frequent releases.

3. **Forking Workflow:** In open-source projects, contributors fork the main repository, create their branches, and submit pull requests. Project maintainers review and merge changes.

## Setting Up Git for Collaboration

To begin collaborating with Git, follow these essential steps:

1. **Install Git:** If you haven't already, download and install Git on your local machine. You can find installation instructions for various platforms on the official Git website.

2. **Configure Git:** Set up your Git identity by configuring your name and email address using the `git config` command. This information appears in your commit history.

3. **Clone a Repository:** To work on an existing project, clone the repository from a remote server using the `git clone` command. This creates a local copy of the project on your machine.

4. **Create Branches:** Create a new branch using `git checkout -b <branch-name>` to isolate your work from the main codebase.

5. **Make Commits:** Make changes to your project files and commit them using `git commit -m "Your commit message"`.

6. **Push and Pull:** Push your changes to a remote repository with `git push` and fetch updates from the remote using `git pull`.

7. **Collaborate and Review:** Collaborate with team members by creating pull requests, reviewing code changes, and discussing improvements.

Git's flexibility and robustness make it an invaluable tool for collaborative coding. Whether you're working on open-source projects or within a development team, mastering Git can greatly enhance your ability to work together efficiently and productively. In the next sections, we'll explore advanced Git topics and best practices for team development.

---

## Section 16.3: Best Practices for Team Development

Effective collaboration in software development involves not only using the right tools like Git but also adhering to best practices that ensure a smooth workflow, high code quality, and productive teamwork. In this section, we'll explore some of the best practices for team development that will help you and your team work efficiently and produce high-quality software.

### 1. Clear and Consistent Code Style

Maintaining a consistent code style across the project is crucial for readability and collaboration. Use coding standards and style guides, and consider adopting code linters and formatters. Popular languages often have tools like ESLint for JavaScript, Pylint for Python, and Checkstyle for Java to enforce coding standards.

### 2. Version Control Etiquette

When working with Git or any version control system, follow etiquette guidelines. Commit small, logical changes with descriptive commit messages. Avoid committing commented-out code or large binary files that don't belong in the repository. Communicate with your team about branch and commit naming conventions.

### 3. Code Reviews

Code reviews are essential for maintaining code quality. Encourage peer reviews for every change. Reviews should focus on correctness, code style, and adherence to project guidelines. Use tools like GitHub Pull Requests or GitLab Merge Requests to facilitate code reviews.

### 4. Automated Testing

Implement automated testing as part of your development process. Write unit tests, integration tests, and end-to-end tests to catch issues early. Continuous Integration (CI) tools like Jenkins, Travis CI, or GitHub Actions can automatically run tests on each code change.

## 5. Documentation

Proper documentation is essential for onboarding new team members and maintaining the project in the long run. Document code, APIs, configuration, and project architecture. Consider using tools like Sphinx for Python or Javadoc for Java to generate documentation.

## 6. Use of Branching Strategies

Adopt a branching strategy that suits your project's needs. Common strategies include feature branching, Gitflow, or trunk-based development. Choose one that aligns with your workflow and project requirements.

## 7. Continuous Integration and Deployment (CI/CD)

Implement CI/CD pipelines to automate building, testing, and deployment processes. This ensures that changes are thoroughly tested and can be deployed to production with confidence. Services like Jenkins, Travis CI, and CircleCI offer robust CI/CD capabilities.

## 8. Communication

Effective communication is vital for a successful team. Use collaboration tools like Slack, Microsoft Teams, or Discord for real-time communication. Document important decisions and discussions in project wikis or documentation.

## 9. Security Best Practices

Security should be a top priority. Regularly update dependencies to patch vulnerabilities, implement security scanning tools, and educate the team about security best practices. Consider using tools like OWASP Dependency-Check for vulnerability scanning.

## 10. Code Ownership and Responsibility

Clearly define code ownership and responsibilities within the team. Encourage team members to take ownership of specific parts of the codebase. This helps in accountability and ensures that code is well-maintained.

## 11. Continuous Learning

Promote a culture of continuous learning. Encourage team members to stay updated with the latest industry trends, tools, and best practices. This can include attending conferences, online courses, or internal knowledge sharing sessions.

## 12. Feedback and Retrospectives

Regularly conduct retrospectives to reflect on what's working well and what can be improved in your development process. Collect feedback from team members and stakeholders to make informed adjustments.

By implementing these best practices, you can foster a collaborative and productive environment within your development team. Effective teamwork and adherence to these principles will result in higher-quality software and a more satisfying development experience.

---

## Section 16.4: Code Reviews and Quality Assurance

Code reviews play a pivotal role in maintaining code quality, identifying issues, and ensuring that your software project remains on track. In this section, we will delve into the importance of code reviews and explore best practices for conducting effective code reviews.

### Why Code Reviews Matter

Code reviews are a systematic examination of code changes by one or more developers, often before those changes are merged into the main codebase. They offer several benefits:

1. **Bug Detection:** Code reviews help catch and fix bugs, logic errors, and other issues before they make their way into production.

2. **Knowledge Sharing:** Code reviews provide opportunities for team members to learn from one another. They facilitate knowledge transfer and cross-training.

3. **Code Consistency:** Code reviews ensure that the codebase adheres to coding standards and style guidelines, maintaining a consistent codebase.

4. **Quality Assurance:** By reviewing code, teams can assess code quality, performance, and security aspects of the changes.

5. **Alignment with Goals:** Code reviews help ensure that the changes align with project goals, requirements, and architecture.

### Best Practices for Code Reviews

To make the most out of code reviews, consider the following best practices:

1. **Establish Code Review Guidelines:** Define clear guidelines for conducting code reviews. These guidelines should cover what aspects to focus on, the expected level of detail, and the etiquette for providing feedback.

2. **Conduct Regular Reviews:** Make code reviews a regular part of your development process. It's better to have smaller, frequent reviews than infrequent, large ones.

3. **Involve Multiple Reviewers:** Involving multiple team members in the review process brings diverse perspectives and helps identify issues more effectively.

4. **Automate with Tools:** Utilize code review tools and platforms like GitHub, GitLab, or Bitbucket. These tools streamline the review process, track changes, and allow discussions.

5. **Keep Reviews Small:** Review smaller, manageable portions of code rather than large changesets. Smaller reviews are more focused and easier to handle.

6. **Provide Constructive Feedback:** When providing feedback, be constructive and specific. Point out issues clearly, suggest solutions, and maintain a positive tone.

7. **Prioritize High-Impact Issues:** Focus on critical issues, such as security vulnerabilities or functionality gaps, first. Address less critical issues afterward.

8. **Use Code Linters and Static Analysis:** Implement code linters and static analysis tools to catch common issues automatically. These tools can save time during reviews.

9. **Balance Speed and Thoroughness:** Aim for a balance between a thorough review and timely delivery. Prioritize critical reviews while keeping the development pace steady.

10. **Document Decisions:** Keep records of review decisions and discussions. This documentation can serve as a reference and provide insights into past decisions.

11. **Learn from Feedback:** Developers should view code reviews as learning opportunities. Accept feedback gracefully and use it to improve your coding skills.

12. **Follow Up:** After addressing review comments, ensure that the changes are re-reviewed to confirm that issues have been resolved correctly.

13. **Consider Pair Programming:** Pair programming is an alternative to traditional code reviews where two developers work together simultaneously. It can reduce the need for subsequent reviews.

14. **Automate Tests:** Integrate automated testing into your CI/CD pipeline. Automated tests provide an additional layer of assurance beyond manual reviews.

15. **Review Non-Functional Aspects:** In addition to code correctness, pay attention to non-functional aspects like performance, security, and scalability.

Effective code reviews contribute significantly to code quality, team collaboration, and overall project success. By following these best practices, you can establish a robust code review process that enhances the quality and reliability of your software.

---

## Section 16.5: Managing Large Codebases Across Teams

Managing large codebases across multiple teams or even organizations can be a daunting task. In this section, we will explore strategies and best practices for effectively handling large-scale codebases, ensuring collaboration, and maintaining code quality.

Large codebases come with a unique set of challenges:

1. **Complexity:** As code grows, it tends to become more complex, making it harder to understand and maintain.

2. **Team Coordination:** Coordinating efforts across multiple teams or developers can be challenging, leading to conflicts and inefficiencies.

3. **Consistency:** Maintaining coding standards and style consistency becomes more critical as the codebase grows.

4. **Performance:** Large codebases can suffer from performance issues, slowing down development and impacting user experience.

5. **Testing and Debugging:** Testing and debugging become more time-consuming and complex as the codebase expands.

## Strategies for Managing Large Codebases

To address these challenges, consider the following strategies:

1. **Modularization:** Break the codebase into smaller, manageable modules. Each module should have a well-defined purpose and interface, making it easier to work on and test.

2. **Version Control:** Use a version control system (e.g., Git) to track changes, collaborate, and manage branches effectively. Branching strategies like GitFlow can help organize development efforts.

3. **Code Reviews:** Continue to emphasize code reviews, even with larger teams. Code reviews help maintain code quality and ensure consistency.

4. **Coding Standards:** Enforce coding standards and style guidelines rigorously. Use linters and code formatters to automate adherence to these standards.

5. **Documentation:** Maintain comprehensive documentation for the codebase. Include high-level architecture diagrams, module-level documentation, and inline comments where necessary.

6. **Automated Testing:** Implement a robust automated testing strategy. Include unit tests, integration tests, and end-to-end tests to catch issues early.

7. **Continuous Integration (CI):** Set up CI pipelines to automate build, test, and deployment processes. CI ensures that changes are tested automatically and consistently.

8. **Monitoring and Profiling:** Implement monitoring and profiling tools to detect performance bottlenecks and issues in real-time.

9. **Code Ownership:** Assign code ownership to specific teams or individuals. Each team is responsible for maintaining their designated parts of the codebase.

10. **Cross-Functional Teams:** Encourage cross-functional teams with members from different domains (e.g., development, QA, operations) to collaborate on features and bug fixes.

11. **Sprint Planning:** Adopt Agile methodologies like Scrum or Kanban to plan and manage development sprints effectively.

12. **Codebase Health Metrics:** Monitor codebase health metrics such as code churn, cyclomatic complexity, and test coverage. Identify areas that need improvement.

13. **Refactoring:** Regularly allocate time for refactoring and code cleanup. Address technical debt to prevent it from accumulating.

14. **Code Audits:** Conduct periodic code audits to identify architectural issues, performance bottlenecks, and potential security vulnerabilities.

15. **Communication:** Foster clear and open communication channels among teams. Regularly update documentation and hold knowledge-sharing sessions.

16. **Scaling Infrastructure:** Ensure that the infrastructure, including servers and databases, can handle the demands of a growing codebase.

17. **Error Handling and Logging:** Implement robust error handling and logging mechanisms to capture issues and diagnose problems effectively.

18. **Security:** Maintain a strong focus on security, including regular security audits and vulnerability assessments.

Managing large codebases is an ongoing process that requires vigilance and adaptability. By implementing these strategies, you can keep your codebase maintainable, ensure code quality, and support the collaborative efforts of multiple teams working on the same project.

# Chapter 17: Optimization and Performance Tuning

## Section 17.1: Analyzing and Improving Code Performance

In this section, we will explore the essential concepts of code optimization and performance tuning. Performance is a critical aspect of software development, impacting user experience, resource consumption, and overall system efficiency. Therefore, it is crucial to understand how to analyze and optimize code for better performance.

### The Importance of Code Performance

Performance tuning is about making your code run faster, use fewer resources, and respond more efficiently to user interactions. There are several reasons why code performance is essential:

1. **User Experience:** Slow and unresponsive applications can frustrate users and lead to a negative perception of your software.

2. **Resource Efficiency:** Optimized code consumes fewer system resources, such as CPU and memory, reducing operational costs.

3. **Scalability:** Performance improvements allow your application to handle more users or data without a proportional increase in resources.

4. **Competitive Advantage:** Faster applications can give your business a competitive edge by providing a superior user experience.

### Profiling and Analysis

Profiling is the process of measuring and analyzing a program's runtime behavior. It helps identify bottlenecks and performance issues in your code. Here are common profiling techniques:

- **CPU Profiling:** Analyzes CPU usage to identify functions or code segments consuming excessive processing time.

- **Memory Profiling:** Detects memory leaks, excessive memory usage, and inefficient memory management.

- **Network Profiling:** Analyzes network communication for latency and inefficiencies.

- **I/O Profiling:** Measures input/output operations, identifying slow file or database accesses.

### Optimization Strategies

Once you've identified performance bottlenecks, you can apply optimization strategies to improve code performance:

1. **Algorithmic Optimization:** Reevaluate algorithms and data structures for efficiency. Sometimes, changing algorithms can lead to significant performance gains.

2. **Code Refactoring:** Restructure code to eliminate redundancy and improve readability. Well-structured code is often more performant.

3. **Parallelism and Concurrency:** Utilize multi-threading or parallel processing to leverage multiple CPU cores.

4. **Caching:** Cache frequently used data or calculations to reduce redundant work.

5. **Lazy Loading:** Load resources or data on-demand instead of loading everything upfront.

6. **Reducing I/O Operations:** Minimize file, database, and network operations by batching or caching data.

7. **Minimizing Garbage Collection:** In languages with garbage collection, reduce object creation and manage memory carefully.

8. **Profile-Guided Optimization (PGO):** Use profiling data to guide compiler optimizations, tailoring the executable to specific usage patterns.

9. **Compiler Optimizations:** Enable compiler optimizations to improve generated machine code.

10. **Hardware Acceleration:** Utilize hardware features (e.g., GPU acceleration) for specific tasks.

11. **Load Balancing:** Distribute workloads evenly across resources to prevent bottlenecks.

12. **Database Query Optimization:** Optimize database queries by using appropriate indexes and minimizing joins.

### Continuous Monitoring and Testing

Performance optimization is an ongoing process. After making improvements, it's crucial to monitor your application's performance and conduct regular performance testing to ensure that changes have a positive impact. Automated testing and benchmarking can help track performance over time and identify regressions.

In conclusion, understanding and optimizing code performance are essential skills for software developers. By profiling, analyzing, and applying optimization strategies, you can create software that performs well, meets user expectations, and operates efficiently in various environments.

# Section 17.2: Profiling Tools and Techniques

Profiling tools play a crucial role in identifying performance bottlenecks and optimizing code. These tools provide insights into how a program consumes resources, helping developers pinpoint areas that require improvement. In this section, we'll explore various profiling tools and techniques used in software development.

## Types of Profiling Tools

1. **CPU Profilers:** CPU profiling tools analyze a program's CPU usage over time. They identify which functions or code segments consume the most CPU cycles. Examples include perf for Linux, Instruments for macOS, and Visual Studio's CPU Profiler for Windows.

2. **Memory Profilers:** Memory profiling tools track memory usage, helping developers find memory leaks, inefficient memory allocation, and excessive memory consumption. Popular memory profilers include Valgrind, Xcode's Instruments, and Visual Studio's Memory Profiler.

3. **Code Profilers:** These tools measure the number of times each line of code is executed and how much time is spent in each function. They help identify performance bottlenecks at a granular level. Profilers like Python's cProfile, Go's pprof, and Java's VisualVM fall into this category.

4. **Network Profilers:** Network profiling tools capture network-related information, such as HTTP requests and responses, DNS queries, and network latency. Wireshark, Fiddler, and browser developer tools are examples of network profilers.

5. **I/O Profilers:** I/O profiling tools monitor input/output operations, including file reads/writes and database queries. Tools like strace (Linux), Process Monitor (Windows), and DTrace (macOS and Linux) can help identify I/O bottlenecks.

## Profiling Techniques

1. **Sampling vs. Instrumentation:** Profiling tools use either sampling or instrumentation techniques. Sampling-based profilers periodically sample program state to collect data, while instrumentation-based profilers insert code into the program to track execution. Sampling is less intrusive but may miss short-lived performance issues.

2. **Heap Profiling:** Heap profiling tools analyze memory allocation and deallocation patterns, helping detect memory leaks and inefficient memory use. They provide insights into which parts of the code allocate the most memory.

3. **Tracing:** Tracing profilers capture a detailed log of program events and their timings. This helps visualize the program's execution flow and identify latency issues. strace and DTrace are examples of tracing tools.

4.  **Call Graphs:** Profilers often generate call graphs that illustrate function call hierarchies. These graphs help developers understand how functions are interrelated and which ones contribute to performance problems.

5.  **Flame Graphs:** Flame graphs are visual representations of profiling data that show where time is spent within a program. They help developers quickly identify hotspots in the code.

Profiling Best Practices

*   **Isolate the Problem:** Profiling tools can generate a lot of data. Start by profiling specific areas of your code where you suspect performance issues.

*   **Reproduce the Issue:** Ensure that the performance problem is reproducible before using profiling tools. This makes it easier to verify the effectiveness of optimizations.

*   **Use Multiple Tools:** Different profiling tools provide complementary insights. Combine the results from CPU, memory, and code profilers to get a holistic view of performance.

*   **Profile Under Real Conditions:** Profiling in a production-like environment is essential because performance can vary based on factors like hardware and network conditions.

*   **Iterate and Test:** After making optimizations based on profiling data, re-run tests and profile again to validate improvements.

*   **Regular Profiling:** Profiling should be part of your development workflow. Regularly profile your code to catch performance regressions early.

Profiling is a powerful technique for optimizing software performance. By using the right profiling tools and techniques, developers can identify bottlenecks, reduce resource consumption, and deliver faster and more efficient applications to users.

---

## Section 17.3: Memory Optimization Strategies

Memory optimization is a critical aspect of software development, as inefficient memory usage can lead to performance issues and even application crashes. In this section, we'll explore various memory optimization strategies and best practices that can help developers write more memory-efficient code.

1. Data Structures Selection

Choosing the right data structure can significantly impact memory usage. Use data structures that minimize memory overhead. For example, if you need a dynamic collection of elements in C++, consider using std::vector instead of std::list for lower memory consumption.

## 2. Object Pooling

Object pooling involves reusing objects instead of creating new ones. This can reduce memory fragmentation and allocation overhead. It's particularly useful for frequently created and destroyed objects, such as bullets in a game or database connections.

```python
# Python example using an object pool
class Bullet:
    def __init__(self):
        self.active = False

# Object pool
bullet_pool = [Bullet() for _ in range(100)]

# Reuse bullets
def fire_bullet():
    for bullet in bullet_pool:
        if not bullet.active:
            bullet.active = True
            return bullet
```

## 3. Lazy Loading

Lazy loading is a technique where data is loaded into memory only when it's needed. This is especially useful when dealing with large datasets. Loading data lazily can reduce the initial memory footprint of an application.

## 4. Memory-Mapped Files

Memory-mapped files allow portions of a file to be mapped directly into memory. This can be beneficial when working with large files because it minimizes the need for reading the entire file into memory. Languages like C and C++ provide memory-mapped file APIs.

## 5. Garbage Collection Optimization

For languages with garbage collectors like Java and Python, understanding how garbage collection works and minimizing unnecessary object retention can improve memory usage. Avoid creating too many short-lived objects, as they can lead to frequent garbage collection.

## 6. Memory Profiling

Use memory profiling tools to identify memory leaks and areas of high memory consumption in your application. Tools like Valgrind (C/C++), Python's memory profiler (memory_profiler), and Visual Studio's Memory Profiler (C#) can help in this regard.

## 7. Dispose of Resources Properly

In languages with manual memory management like C and C++, it's crucial to release allocated memory and other resources when they are no longer needed. Failing to do so can result in memory leaks.

```
// C example - free allocated memory
int* numbers = (int*)malloc(100 * sizeof(int));
// Use the allocated memory
free(numbers); // Release the memory when done
```

## 8. Minimize Copying

Avoid unnecessary copying of data, especially with large objects. Use references or pointers where appropriate to avoid duplicating data in memory. In languages like C++, move semantics can help reduce copying.

## 9. Compact Data Structures

Compact data structures use less memory to represent the same information. For example, using bitsets or packed arrays to store boolean flags can save memory compared to using individual boolean variables.

## 10. Monitoring and Profiling

Regularly monitor your application's memory usage and profile it to detect memory-related issues. Profiling tools can provide valuable insights into memory allocation patterns and potential optimizations.

Memory optimization is an ongoing process that requires careful consideration throughout the development lifecycle. By implementing these strategies and regularly profiling your code, you can create more memory-efficient software that delivers better performance and user experience.

---

## Section 17.4: Optimizing CPU Usage and Efficiency

Efficient CPU usage is crucial for the performance of software applications. In this section, we'll explore strategies and techniques to optimize CPU usage and improve the efficiency of your code.

## 1. Algorithm Selection

Choosing the right algorithm for a specific task can significantly impact CPU usage. Analyze the time complexity of algorithms and select the one that provides the desired functionality with the least computational overhead. For example, use quicksort instead of bubblesort for sorting large datasets.

```python
# Python example - Sorting with quicksort
def quicksort(arr):
    if len(arr) <= 1:
        return arr
    pivot = arr[len(arr) // 2]
    left = [x for x in arr if x < pivot]
```

```
    middle = [x for x in arr if x == pivot]
    right = [x for x in arr if x > pivot]
    return quicksort(left) + middle + quicksort(right)
```

## 2. Data Structure Optimization

Efficient data structures can reduce CPU usage. Choose data structures that provide fast access and manipulation times. For example, use hash tables for fast key-value lookups and dynamic arrays for constant-time random access.

## 3. Caching

Caching involves storing frequently accessed data in a fast-access memory location. This reduces the need to recalculate or retrieve data from slower sources, such as databases or remote servers. Caching can significantly improve application responsiveness and reduce CPU usage.

```
// Java example - Using a cache
import java.util.HashMap;
import java.util.Map;

public class DataCache {
    private Map<String, String> cache = new HashMap<>();

    public String fetchData(String key) {
        if (cache.containsKey(key)) {
            return cache.get(key);
        } else {
            // Fetch data from the source
            String data = fetchDataFromSource(key);
            cache.put(key, data);
            return data;
        }
    }

    private String fetchDataFromSource(String key) {
        // Simulate fetching data from a source
        return "Data for " + key;
    }
}
```

## 4. Multithreading and Parallelism

Utilize multithreading and parallelism to distribute CPU-intensive tasks across multiple threads or processors. This can lead to significant performance improvements for applications that perform tasks concurrently.

### 5. Profile and Optimize Hotspots

Use profiling tools to identify performance bottlenecks or "hotspots" in your code. Once identified, focus on optimizing these areas by using more efficient algorithms or data structures. Profiling tools can provide insights into which parts of your code consume the most CPU time.

### 6. Batch Processing

For tasks that involve processing a large number of items, consider batch processing. Instead of processing items one by one, process them in batches. This can reduce overhead and improve CPU efficiency.

### 7. Compiler and Language Features

Leverage compiler optimizations and language-specific features designed to improve code efficiency. For example, in C and C++, you can use compiler flags like -O2 or -O3 to enable optimization levels. In Java, you can use the final keyword to allow the JVM to apply certain optimizations.

### 8. Minimize I/O Operations

I/O operations, such as reading from or writing to disk, are often slower than CPU operations. Minimize unnecessary I/O by caching data, batching I/O requests, and optimizing file access patterns.

### 9. Use Lazy Evaluation

Lazy evaluation is a technique where expressions are not evaluated until their results are needed. This can reduce unnecessary computations. Functional languages like Haskell and languages with functional features like Python's generators utilize lazy evaluation.

Optimizing CPU usage is an essential part of software development, especially for applications that require high performance and responsiveness. By employing these strategies and continuously profiling and measuring the performance of your code, you can ensure that your software runs efficiently and meets its performance goals.

---

## Section 17.5: Balancing Readability and Performance

Balancing readability and performance is a crucial aspect of software development. While optimizing code for performance is essential, it should not come at the cost of code readability and maintainability. In this section, we'll explore strategies for achieving a balance between these two important aspects.

## 1. Code Comments and Documentation

Maintaining clear and concise code comments and documentation is essential for readability. Describe the purpose of functions, classes, and complex algorithms. When optimizing code, ensure that you update comments to reflect any changes.

```python
# Python example - Adding code comments
def calculate_total(items):
    """
    Calculate the total cost of items in a shopping cart.

    Args:
        items (list): List of item prices.

    Returns:
        float: Total cost.
    """
    total = sum(items)
    return total
```

## 2. Descriptive Variable and Function Names

Use descriptive variable and function names that convey their purpose. Avoid single-letter variable names or overly abbreviated names. Clear names make it easier for other developers (and your future self) to understand the code.

```javascript
// JavaScript example - Descriptive variable names
function calculateAreaOfRectangle(length, width) {
    return length * width;
}
```

## 3. Modularization

Break your code into smaller, manageable modules or functions. Each module should have a single responsibility, making it easier to understand and maintain. This also facilitates code reuse.

```java
// Java example - Modularization
public class Calculator {
    public static int add(int a, int b) {
        return a + b;
    }

    public static int subtract(int a, int b) {
        return a - b;
    }
}
```

## 4. Code Formatting and Style Guides

Consistent code formatting and adherence to style guides contribute to readability. Use automated code formatting tools and follow established coding conventions for your programming language.

## 5. Avoid Premature Optimization

Don't optimize code prematurely. Focus on writing clear, correct, and maintainable code first. Afterward, use profiling tools to identify performance bottlenecks and optimize only where necessary.

## 6. Maintainability over Micro-Optimizations

Optimizations at the micro-level (e.g., loop unrolling) can improve performance but often make code less readable. Prioritize maintainability over micro-optimizations unless they are critical for your application's performance.

## 7. Code Reviews

Regular code reviews involving peers can help maintain code quality. Reviewers can provide feedback on code readability and suggest improvements.

## 8. Testing and Test-Driven Development (TDD)

Unit tests and TDD ensure that code functions correctly and helps prevent regressions when optimizing. Tests also serve as documentation, showcasing how functions should be used.

```python
# Python example - Writing unit tests
import unittest

def add(a, b):
    return a + b

class TestAddFunction(unittest.TestCase):
    def test_add_positive_numbers(self):
        self.assertEqual(add(2, 3), 5)

    def test_add_negative_numbers(self):
        self.assertEqual(add(-2, -3), -5)

if __name__ == '__main__':
    unittest.main()
```

## 9. Code Refactoring

Periodically revisit and refactor code to improve both readability and performance. Refactoring can lead to better-designed, more maintainable code that remains efficient.

Balancing readability and performance is an ongoing process. Remember that optimizing for readability should be the default approach, and optimizations should be made judiciously based on performance profiling and real-world needs. Striking the right balance will result in code that is not only performant but also understandable and maintainable by your development team.

---

# Chapter 18: The Future of Programming Languages

## Section 18.1: Emerging Trends in Software Development

The world of software development is dynamic, and programming languages play a central role in shaping the future of this field. In this section, we will explore some of the emerging trends in software development and the programming languages that are at the forefront of these innovations.

### 1. Machine Learning Integration

Machine learning and artificial intelligence (AI) have gained significant traction in recent years. Programming languages like Python and libraries like TensorFlow and PyTorch have made it easier for developers to integrate machine learning into their applications. The future will likely see even more seamless integration of ML capabilities into programming languages, making it accessible to a broader range of developers.

### 2. Quantum Computing Languages

Quantum computing is on the horizon, and with it comes the need for specialized programming languages. Languages like Q# (pronounced Q-sharp) are already being developed to address the unique challenges of quantum computing. As quantum computers become more accessible, these languages will play a crucial role in harnessing their power.

### 3. WebAssembly (Wasm)

WebAssembly is a binary instruction format that enables high-performance execution of code on web browsers. While not a programming language in itself, it opens up possibilities for using multiple languages for web development. This trend is likely to continue as developers explore new languages that compile to Wasm, expanding the choices for web application development.

### 4. Rust for System-Level Programming

Rust is gaining popularity as a language for system-level programming due to its focus on safety, performance, and concurrency. As security and performance continue to be critical concerns in software development, Rust's adoption is expected to grow, especially in industries where reliability is paramount, such as autonomous vehicles and aerospace.

### 5. Domain-Specific Languages (DSLs)

Domain-specific languages tailored for specific industries or use cases are becoming more prevalent. These languages are designed to solve particular problems efficiently. For example, SQL (Structured Query Language) is a DSL for database querying. The future will likely see an increase in the creation of DSLs for various specialized domains.

## 6. Low-Code and No-Code Platforms

Low-code and no-code platforms are simplifying application development by enabling users to create software with minimal coding effort. While these platforms do not replace traditional programming languages, they are changing the landscape by allowing non-developers to participate in software creation. The future may bring more innovation in this area, making software development even more accessible.

## 7. Concurrency and Parallelism

With the advent of multi-core processors, concurrency and parallelism are becoming increasingly important. Programming languages are evolving to provide better support for concurrent and parallel programming. Go (Golang), for example, was designed with concurrency in mind. Future languages may incorporate similar features to simplify concurrent programming.

## 8. Ethical and Sustainable Programming

As technology's impact on society grows, there is a growing emphasis on ethical and sustainable programming practices. Programming languages and tools that help developers build ethical AI systems, reduce energy consumption, and minimize environmental impact will likely gain prominence.

## 9. Continued Evolution of Existing Languages

Existing programming languages like Python, JavaScript, and Rust will continue to evolve to meet the changing needs of developers. Language maintainers and the open-source community will introduce new features and improvements, ensuring the longevity and relevance of these languages.

## 10. Interoperability

In a connected world, interoperability between different programming languages and systems is crucial. Languages that facilitate easy integration and communication between diverse components will be favored. This trend will promote the use of APIs, microservices, and standardized data formats.

In conclusion, the future of programming languages is marked by innovation, adaptability, and responsiveness to emerging trends in technology and software development. Developers and organizations should stay informed about these trends to make informed decisions about language adoption and to remain competitive in the ever-evolving world of software engineering.

## Section 18.2: The Evolution of Programming Paradigms

Programming paradigms are fundamental approaches to solving problems through software development. Over the years, various paradigms have emerged, evolved, and shaped the way we think about and write code. In this section, we will explore the evolution of programming paradigms and their impact on the languages we use.

### 1. Procedural Programming

Procedural programming, characterized by the use of procedures or functions, was one of the earliest paradigms. Languages like Fortran and COBOL were pioneers in this regard. Developers wrote code as a sequence of procedures, making it easier to structure and organize programs.

### 2. Object-Oriented Programming (OOP)

OOP emerged in the 1960s and gained prominence with languages like Smalltalk and later, C++. OOP focuses on organizing code into objects that encapsulate data and behavior. This paradigm introduced concepts like classes, inheritance, and polymorphism, making code more modular and reusable.

```python
class Animal:
    def __init__(self, name):
        self.name = name

    def speak(self):
        pass

class Dog(Animal):
    def speak(self):
        return "Woof!"

class Cat(Animal):
    def speak(self):
        return "Meow!"

dog = Dog("Buddy")
cat = Cat("Whiskers")

print(dog.speak())   # Output: Woof!
print(cat.speak())   # Output: Meow!
```

### 3. Functional Programming

Functional programming, rooted in lambda calculus, emphasizes immutability and the use of pure functions. Languages like Lisp and Haskell exemplify this paradigm. Functional programming languages treat computation as the evaluation of mathematical functions, which can lead to concise and predictable code.

194

```haskell
-- Haskell example
square :: Int -> Int
square x = x * x

main :: IO ()
main = do
    let numbers = [1, 2, 3, 4, 5]
    let squares = map square numbers
    print squares   -- Output: [1, 4, 9, 16, 25]
```

## 4. Logic Programming

Logic programming, epitomized by Prolog, revolves around defining rules and relationships in a declarative manner. Developers specify what should be achieved rather than how to achieve it. This paradigm is commonly used in fields like artificial intelligence and natural language processing.

```prolog
% Prolog example
mortal(X) :- human(X).
human(socrates).

?- mortal(socrates).
% Output: true
```

## 5. Event-Driven and Reactive Programming

With the rise of graphical user interfaces and real-time systems, event-driven and reactive programming paradigms became prominent. Languages like JavaScript and libraries like RxJS enable developers to build applications that respond to events and data streams.

```javascript
// JavaScript example using RxJS
import { fromEvent } from 'rxjs';

const button = document.getElementById('myButton');
const clickObservable = fromEvent(button, 'click');

clickObservable.subscribe(() => {
    console.log('Button clicked!');
});
```

## 6. Concurrent and Parallel Programming

As hardware architectures evolved to include multiple cores, concurrent and parallel programming paradigms became crucial. Languages like Go (Golang) and Erlang offer built-in support for concurrency. These paradigms allow developers to write code that efficiently utilizes the available computing resources.

```go
// Go example
package main
```

```go
import (
    "fmt"
    "sync"
)

func main() {
    var wg sync.WaitGroup
    wg.Add(2)

    go func() {
        defer wg.Done()
        fmt.Println("Goroutine 1")
    }()

    go func() {
        defer wg.Done()
        fmt.Println("Goroutine 2")
    }()

    wg.Wait()
}
```

## 7. Domain-Specific Languages (DSLs)

DSLs are designed for specific domains or tasks. While they are not a separate paradigm, they represent a focused approach to solving particular problems. DSLs are often embedded within other languages and allow developers to express solutions in a more domain-specific and readable way.

```sql
-- SQL (Structured Query Language) example
SELECT name, age FROM employees WHERE department = 'Engineering';
```

## 8. Low-Code and No-Code Paradigms

Low-code and no-code platforms are changing the way software is developed. These paradigms empower individuals with limited coding experience to create applications visually or with minimal scripting. While not traditional programming paradigms, they are reshaping how software solutions are produced.

## 9. Hybrid Approaches

Modern programming often involves mixing and matching paradigms to address complex problems. Languages like Python and JavaScript offer the flexibility to use procedural, OOP, and functional approaches within the same codebase. This hybridization allows developers to choose the best paradigm for each part of their application.

In conclusion, the evolution of programming paradigms reflects

## Section 18.3: Predictions for C, C++, Java, JavaScript, and Python

The world of programming languages is constantly evolving, and while we can't predict the future with absolute certainty, we can make educated guesses about the trajectory of some of the most popular languages. In this section, we'll explore predictions for the future of C, C++, Java, JavaScript, and Python.

### 1. C and C++

C and C++ have a long-standing history and are known for their performance and system-level programming capabilities. While these languages might not see radical changes, they will likely continue to evolve to meet the demands of modern software development.

In the case of C, it is expected to remain a staple in embedded systems, operating systems, and low-level programming. It will likely receive updates for better support of modern hardware and security features.

C++ will likely continue its evolution toward a more modern and expressive language while maintaining backward compatibility. Features like modules, concepts, and smart pointers introduced in recent standards will become more widespread.

### 2. Java

Java, with its "Write Once, Run Anywhere" promise, will continue to be relevant in the enterprise world. It is expected to adapt to new trends, such as microservices architecture and cloud-native development.

The release cycle of Java has accelerated with the introduction of a new version every six months. This allows Java to incorporate new features and improvements more quickly. Project Valhalla, Panama, and Loom are expected to bring significant enhancements to performance, native interop, and concurrency.

### 3. JavaScript

JavaScript's dominance in web development is unlikely to wane. It will continue to evolve with a focus on making web applications more efficient, secure, and maintainable.

The rise of WebAssembly will allow JavaScript to extend its reach to tasks traditionally performed by other languages, like C and C++. JavaScript engines will further optimize the execution of WebAssembly code.

Frameworks and libraries like React, Angular, and Vue.js will continue to shape the way web applications are built, providing developers with powerful tools for building dynamic and responsive user interfaces.

### 4. Python

Python's popularity is expected to grow further, driven by its simplicity, readability, and versatility. It will continue to be a dominant language in data science, machine learning, and artificial intelligence.

Python's performance will improve with the adoption of features like static typing through tools like "TypeScript." Python 4.x is anticipated to address backward-incompatible changes while introducing new language features.

Web frameworks like Django and Flask will see enhancements, making Python a viable choice for web development beyond its strength in other domains.

### 5. Cross-Language Interoperability

One trend that is likely to become more prominent is the interoperability between languages. Developers will increasingly use multiple languages in a single project, choosing the best tool for each task. Technologies like WebAssembly and language-agnostic interfaces will facilitate this trend.

### 6. The Impact of AI

Artificial intelligence (AI) will play a significant role in the future of programming languages. AI-driven tools will assist developers in writing code, optimizing performance, and even detecting and fixing bugs. This will lead to more efficient and reliable software development processes.

In conclusion, while we can't predict every detail of the future, it's clear that programming languages will continue to adapt to meet the evolving needs of developers and the technology landscape. Developers who stay current with these trends will be well-prepared to navigate the ever-changing world of programming languages and create innovative solutions.

---

## Section 18.4: The Role of AI in Programming

Artificial Intelligence (AI) has been making waves in various industries, and programming is no exception. In this section, we'll explore the growing role of AI in programming, including how it's being used, its benefits, and the challenges it presents.

### 1. Automated Code Generation

AI is being employed to automatically generate code snippets, functions, and even entire programs. Tools like OpenAI's GPT-3 have demonstrated the ability to write code in response to natural language descriptions. This can significantly speed up development and reduce the need for repetitive coding tasks.

For example, a developer can describe a function's behavior, and AI can generate the code that implements it. While this is a promising development, it's important to ensure the generated code is correct, efficient, and secure.

## 2. Code Review and Quality Assurance

AI-powered code review tools are becoming more sophisticated. They can identify coding style violations, potential bugs, and security vulnerabilities. These tools provide immediate feedback to developers, helping them write cleaner and more reliable code.

Some AI systems can even suggest fixes for identified issues. For instance, they might propose more efficient algorithms or point out potential null pointer exceptions. This assistance can significantly improve code quality and reduce debugging efforts.

## 3. Bug Detection and Predictive Maintenance

AI can analyze codebases to identify potential bugs or areas of code that are prone to issues. By analyzing patterns in code and historical bug data, AI can predict where problems might occur and suggest preemptive fixes. This can be particularly valuable in large and complex software projects.

In addition, AI can help with predictive maintenance by analyzing logs and usage patterns to anticipate and prevent system failures or performance degradation. This proactive approach can minimize downtime and improve user experience.

## 4. Optimizing Code Performance

AI can be used to optimize code performance. Machine learning algorithms can profile code execution and suggest improvements to enhance speed and efficiency. This is particularly valuable in applications where performance is critical, such as gaming, high-frequency trading, or scientific simulations.

AI-driven performance optimization can involve anything from recommending algorithmic improvements to suggesting compiler flags for better code generation.

## 5. Natural Language Interfaces for Coding

AI-powered natural language interfaces are becoming more prevalent. Developers can interact with code using plain English or other natural languages, and AI interprets their intent and generates the corresponding code.

For example, a developer could say, "Create a function that sorts an array in ascending order," and AI would generate the sorting function. This approach lowers the barrier to entry for programming and makes it more accessible to non-technical stakeholders.

## 6. Challenges and Ethical Considerations

While AI brings many benefits to programming, it also presents challenges. Ensuring the correctness of AI-generated code is crucial, as errors can have serious consequences. Developers must review and test AI-generated code thoroughly.

Ethical considerations, such as bias in AI models and the potential for job displacement, also need to be addressed. Developers and organizations must use AI responsibly and consider the broader implications of its use.

In conclusion, AI is becoming an integral part of the programming landscape. It offers the potential to improve productivity, code quality, and software performance. However, its adoption must be accompanied by rigorous testing, ethical considerations, and a commitment to responsible use. As AI continues to advance, it will likely reshape how we approach programming and software development.

---

## Section 18.5: Preparing for the Next Generation of Languages

As the world of technology evolves at a rapid pace, so do programming languages. In this section, we'll discuss how developers can prepare for the next generation of programming languages, anticipate emerging trends, and adapt to the changing landscape of software development.

### 1. Stay Informed

To prepare for the next generation of programming languages, developers must stay informed about the latest developments in the field. This includes keeping an eye on emerging languages, language extensions, and new paradigms. Subscribing to industry news, blogs, and forums can help developers stay up-to-date.

### 2. Learn Multiple Paradigms

Programming paradigms continue to evolve, with functional programming, reactive programming, and other paradigms gaining popularity. Learning multiple paradigms can make developers more adaptable and capable of leveraging the strengths of different languages and paradigms for specific tasks.

### 3. Master Fundamentals

While languages and paradigms may change, fundamental concepts like data structures, algorithms, and software design principles remain essential. A strong foundation in these areas will always be valuable, regardless of the programming language in use.

### 4. Experiment with New Languages

Exploring new programming languages, even if they haven't yet gained widespread adoption, can be beneficial. Experimenting with new languages allows developers to broaden their horizons, gain insights into different approaches, and discover innovative solutions to problems.

## 5. Open Source Contribution

Engaging in open source projects related to programming languages is a great way to gain hands-on experience and contribute to the development of new languages and tools. It also provides an opportunity to collaborate with experts and learn from their expertise.

## 6. Adopt Modern Development Practices

Modern development practices like DevOps, continuous integration and continuous delivery (CI/CD), and agile methodologies are essential for staying competitive in the software industry. Developers should embrace these practices to remain agile and responsive to change.

## 7. Cross-Platform Development

As the demand for cross-platform applications grows, developers should explore languages and frameworks that facilitate cross-platform development. This includes languages like Rust and frameworks like Flutter. Being proficient in cross-platform development can open up new opportunities.

## 8. Consider Domain-Specific Languages (DSLs)

Domain-specific languages tailored for specific industries or problem domains are on the rise. Developers should be open to learning and creating DSLs when they are the most effective solution for a particular task.

## 9. Ethical Considerations

Developers should also consider the ethical implications of the languages they use and the software they build. Ethical considerations, such as privacy, security, and accessibility, are increasingly important, and developers should prioritize responsible and ethical coding practices.

## 10. Foster a Growth Mindset

Finally, adopting a growth mindset is crucial. Embrace change, view challenges as opportunities to learn, and be open to exploring new ideas and technologies. The ability to adapt and evolve will be a key asset as programming languages and software development continue to evolve.

In conclusion, preparing for the next generation of programming languages requires a proactive and adaptable approach. Developers should invest in continuous learning, stay informed about industry trends, and be open to experimentation. By mastering fundamentals, embracing modern practices, and considering ethical implications, developers can position themselves for success in a dynamic and ever-changing field.

## Section 19.1: Case Studies of Successful Projects in Each Language

In this section, we will delve into case studies of successful software projects implemented in various programming languages, highlighting how each language's unique features and strengths contributed to the success of these projects. These real-world examples demonstrate the practical applications of programming languages and the impact they can have on the development of innovative solutions.

### 1. Linux Kernel (C)

The Linux operating system kernel, written in C, stands as one of the most prominent open-source projects in the world. C's low-level capabilities and portability were crucial in developing an operating system that runs on a wide range of hardware architectures. Its performance, reliability, and scalability have made it the backbone of many computing systems, from embedded devices to data centers.

```c
#include <stdio.h>

int main() {
    printf("Hello, Linux!\n");
    return 0;
}
```

### 2. Facebook (PHP and Hack)

Facebook, one of the largest social media platforms, initially used PHP for its web development. As the platform grew, Facebook developed Hack, a statically typed language that interoperates seamlessly with PHP. This combination allowed rapid development of dynamic web applications while maintaining a high degree of type safety.

```php
<?php
echo "Hello, Facebook!";
?>
```

### 3. Netflix (Java)

Netflix, a streaming giant, relies on Java for its backend infrastructure and various microservices. Java's platform independence and robust ecosystem, along with technologies like Spring Boot, have enabled Netflix to deliver high-quality streaming services to millions of users worldwide.

```java
public class HelloWorld {
    public static void main(String[] args) {
        System.out.println("Hello, Netflix!");
    }
}
```

## 4. Twitter (Scala)

Twitter adopted Scala, a language that combines object-oriented and functional programming features, to enhance the performance and maintainability of its systems. Scala's conciseness and compatibility with Java libraries made it an excellent choice for building highly concurrent and scalable applications.

```scala
object HelloWorld {
  def main(args: Array[String]): Unit = {
    println("Hello, Twitter!")
  }
}
```

## 5. Instagram (Python)

Instagram, a popular photo-sharing platform, utilizes Python for its backend infrastructure. Python's simplicity, readability, and extensive libraries, such as Django and Flask, have expedited the development of Instagram's web services and APIs.

```python
print("Hello, Instagram!")
```

## 6. SpaceX (C++, Python)

SpaceX, a private aerospace manufacturer, uses a combination of C++ and Python for tasks ranging from flight software development to data analysis. C++ provides the low-level control needed for rocket systems, while Python's ease of use and data processing capabilities are leveraged for analysis and simulation.

```cpp
#include <iostream>

int main() {
    std::cout << "Hello, SpaceX!" << std::endl;
    return 0;
}
```

These case studies demonstrate the versatility of programming languages and their suitability for different domains and projects. Each language was chosen based on its strengths and characteristics, emphasizing the importance of selecting the right tool for the job. Successful projects not only rely on skilled developers but also on the strategic choice of programming languages and technologies that align with project requirements and goals.

---

## Section 19.2: Cross-Disciplinary Use of Programming Languages

In this section, we explore how programming languages are not confined to a single domain but are often used across various disciplines to solve complex problems. The adaptability and versatility of programming languages enable professionals in different fields to leverage technology for their specific needs.

1. Bioinformatics (Python and R)

In the field of bioinformatics, researchers analyze biological data, such as DNA sequences and protein structures. Python and R are widely used for tasks like sequence alignment, data visualization, and statistical analysis. Biologists and geneticists benefit from these languages' extensive libraries tailored for biological research.

```python
import numpy as np
import matplotlib.pyplot as plt

# Analyzing DNA sequences
sequence = "ATCGGTA"
gc_content = (sequence.count("G") + sequence.count("C")) / len(sequence)
print(f"GC content: {gc_content}")

# Visualizing data
data = np.random.rand(100)
plt.hist(data, bins=10)
plt.show()
```

2. Finance (Java and C++)

Financial institutions rely on Java and C++ for building high-frequency trading systems and risk management tools. These languages offer the speed and precision required for processing large datasets and executing trades within milliseconds.

```java
public class TradingAlgorithm {
    public static void main(String[] args) {
        // Implementing trading logic in Java
        // ...
    }
}
```

```cpp
#include <iostream>

int main() {
    // Risk assessment in C++
    // ...
    return 0;
}
```

3. Geographic Information Systems (GIS) (Python and JavaScript)

GIS professionals use Python and JavaScript to develop mapping applications and analyze geographic data. Python's libraries, such as Geopandas, simplify geospatial data manipulation, while JavaScript's versatility powers interactive web-based maps.

```python
import geopandas as gpd

# Analyzing geographic data with Python
gdf = gpd.read_file('shapefile.shp')
print(gdf.head())
```

```javascript
// Creating interactive maps with JavaScript
const map = L.map('map').setView([51.505, -0.09], 13);
L.tileLayer('https://{s}.tile.openstreetmap.org/{z}/{x}/{y}.png').addTo(map);
```

4. Artificial Intelligence (AI) (Python and TensorFlow)

AI researchers and practitioners harness Python's simplicity and TensorFlow's power to build machine learning models and neural networks. Python's extensive libraries and frameworks, including TensorFlow and PyTorch, facilitate deep learning and AI development.

```python
import tensorflow as tf

# Creating a neural network in TensorFlow
model = tf.keras.Sequential([
    tf.keras.layers.Dense(64, activation='relu'),
    tf.keras.layers.Dense(10)
])
```

5. Digital Art (Processing and JavaScript)

Artists and creative coders use languages like Processing and JavaScript to create interactive digital art installations. These languages provide tools for visual design and interactivity, allowing artists to blend code with artistic expression.

```javascript
// Creating generative art with JavaScript
// ...
```

These examples illustrate how programming languages transcend traditional boundaries, enabling professionals in various fields to leverage technology for their specific needs. The choice of a programming language often depends on factors like ease of use, libraries available, and the specific requirements of the discipline, highlighting the adaptability of programming languages in a cross-disciplinary context.

---

## Section 19.3: Large-Scale Systems and Their Challenges

Large-scale software systems are prevalent in today's technology landscape, powering everything from social media platforms to financial institutions and cloud services. These systems serve millions, if not billions, of users simultaneously. In this section, we delve into the complexities of large-scale systems and the challenges they pose.

## 1. Scalability

One of the foremost challenges in large-scale systems is scalability. Systems must be designed to handle a growing number of users and data. Scalability can be achieved through techniques such as load balancing, horizontal scaling, and efficient database management.

```
# Load balancing in a web application
# ...
```

## 2. Availability and Reliability

Maintaining high availability and reliability is crucial for large-scale systems. Downtime can result in significant financial losses and user dissatisfaction. Redundancy, failover mechanisms, and distributed architectures are essential components of achieving high availability.

```
// Implementing failover mechanisms in a distributed system
// ...
```

## 3. Data Management

Large-scale systems often deal with vast amounts of data. Efficient data storage, retrieval, and processing are paramount. NoSQL databases like Cassandra and distributed file systems like Hadoop are commonly used for managing massive datasets.

```
// Handling large-scale data processing with Hadoop
// ...
```

## 4. Security and Privacy

With a large user base comes increased security concerns. Large-scale systems are lucrative targets for cyberattacks. Robust security measures, including encryption, access controls, and continuous monitoring, are imperative.

```
# Implementing encryption in a web application
# ...
```

## 5. Performance Optimization

Large-scale systems must be optimized for performance to ensure responsiveness and user satisfaction. Profiling tools, caching mechanisms, and code optimization are essential for achieving high performance.

```cpp
#include <iostream>

int main() {
    // Profiling and optimizing code
    // ...
    return 0;
}
```

## 6. Monitoring and Analytics

Continuous monitoring and analytics are vital for identifying and mitigating issues in large-scale systems. Tools like Prometheus and Grafana enable real-time monitoring and data-driven decision-making.

```
// Setting up monitoring with Prometheus and Grafana
// ...
```

## 7. Cost Management

Running large-scale systems can be expensive. Efficient resource allocation and cost management strategies, such as serverless computing and auto-scaling, help control operational expenses.

```
// Implementing serverless computing for cost optimization
// ...
```

## 8. Maintainability and DevOps

Large-scale systems require frequent updates and maintenance. Adopting DevOps practices, including continuous integration and continuous deployment (CI/CD), streamlines the development and deployment processes.

```
# Implementing CI/CD pipelines for a large-scale application
# ...
```

In conclusion, large-scale systems present unique challenges, from scalability and availability to security and cost management. Addressing these challenges requires careful planning, robust architectural design, and the use of appropriate tools and technologies. As technology continues to advance, the complexity of large-scale systems is likely to increase, making it crucial for organizations to stay updated and proactive in addressing these challenges.

---

## Section 19.4: Open Source Contributions and Community Impact

Open source software development has become an integral part of the tech industry, fostering collaboration, innovation, and community-driven projects. In this section, we explore the significance of open source contributions and their impact on the programming world.

### 1. The Open Source Movement

The open source movement promotes the idea that software should be freely accessible, modifiable, and distributable. This philosophy has given rise to numerous open source projects and communities where developers can collaborate on projects of mutual interest.

## 2. Benefits of Open Source Contributions

Contributing to open source projects offers several benefits to developers and the community:

- **Skill Development:** Developers gain valuable experience by working on real-world projects and collaborating with peers.
- **Community Building:** Open source projects foster a sense of community, where developers can share knowledge and mentor one another.
- **Resume Enhancement:** Contributions to well-known open source projects can enhance a developer's resume and career prospects.
- **Solving Real Problems:** Open source software often addresses real-world problems, allowing contributors to make a meaningful impact.

## 3. Popular Open Source Projects

Many popular programming languages and tools are open source, including Linux, Python, Git, and Node.js. These projects have thriving communities and welcome contributions from developers worldwide.

## 4. Contributing to Open Source

Contributing to open source projects can take various forms:

- **Code Contributions:** Writing, testing, and submitting code changes or bug fixes.
- **Documentation:** Improving project documentation for better accessibility.
- **Issue Reporting:** Identifying and reporting bugs or issues.
- **Community Support:** Assisting other users and developers in community forums.

## 5. GitHub and Collaboration Platforms

GitHub is a widely used platform for hosting open source projects and facilitating collaboration. Developers can fork projects, submit pull requests, and participate in discussions.

```
To fork a GitHub repository and make contributions:

1. Visit the project's repository on GitHub.
2. Click the "Fork" button to create a copy of the repository under your acco
unt.
3. Clone your forked repository to your local machine.
4. Make code changes, commit them, and push to your fork on GitHub.
5. Create a pull request to propose changes to the original project.
6. Collaborate with maintainers and peers to refine and merge your contributi
ons.
```

## 6. Licensing and Legal Considerations

Open source projects typically have licenses that govern how the software can be used, modified, and distributed. Developers should be aware of these licenses to ensure compliance and legal clarity.

## 7. Community Etiquette

When contributing to open source, it's essential to follow community guidelines and etiquette. This includes respecting maintainers' decisions, providing constructive feedback, and adhering to code of conduct standards.

## 8. Impact of Open Source

Open source contributions have had a profound impact on the tech industry, enabling the development of critical software infrastructure and fostering innovation. Many widely used technologies and libraries owe their success to the open source community.

In summary, open source contributions offer a pathway for developers to grow their skills, connect with like-minded individuals, and make a positive impact on the software ecosystem. By participating in open source projects, developers can contribute to the greater good of the programming community while advancing their own knowledge and careers.

---

## Section 19.5: Lessons Learned from Industry Giants

Learning from industry giants in the field of programming is invaluable for both aspiring and experienced developers. In this section, we delve into some of the key lessons that can be drawn from the practices and experiences of prominent tech companies and individuals.

## 1. Continuous Learning and Adaptation

One of the fundamental lessons from industry leaders is the importance of continuous learning and adaptability. Technology evolves rapidly, and those who stay up-to-date with the latest trends, tools, and methodologies tend to thrive. Google, for example, encourages its employees to dedicate 20% of their time to personal projects, fostering innovation and learning.

## 2. User-Centric Design

User-centric design principles emphasize creating products and solutions that cater to the needs and preferences of users. Apple's success is often attributed to its focus on providing a seamless and enjoyable user experience. Prioritizing user feedback and conducting usability testing can significantly enhance the quality of software.

### 3. Iterative Development

Iterative development involves building and improving software incrementally. Agile methodologies, championed by companies like Amazon, promote iterative practices. Breaking projects into smaller, manageable tasks allows for quicker releases, faster feedback, and adaptation to changing requirements.

### 4. Automation and DevOps

Automation is a key driver of efficiency and reliability in software development. Companies like Netflix and Amazon have embraced DevOps practices, combining development and operations to automate processes and ensure rapid, error-free deployments. Implementing automation tools, such as Jenkins and Docker, can streamline development pipelines.

### 5. Data-Driven Decision Making

Data-driven decision making is another critical lesson from industry giants. Google and Facebook, for instance, heavily rely on data analytics to inform product decisions and marketing strategies. Developers should embrace data collection and analysis to optimize their applications and services.

### 6. Scalability and Performance

Building scalable and high-performance systems is essential, especially for companies dealing with massive user bases. Lessons from companies like Twitter and Airbnb emphasize the importance of efficient algorithms, caching mechanisms, and load balancing to handle increased traffic.

### 7. Security and Privacy

Ensuring the security and privacy of user data is paramount. Breaches can have severe consequences, both legally and in terms of reputation. Companies like Microsoft invest heavily in security measures and encourage developers to follow best practices, including regular security audits and code reviews.

### 8. Collaboration and Communication

Effective collaboration and communication are critical in team-based software development. Tech giants like Microsoft and Google emphasize clear communication channels, regular meetings, and the use of collaboration tools such as Slack and Microsoft Teams to facilitate teamwork.

### 9. Diversity and Inclusion

Promoting diversity and inclusion is a lesson from industry giants that is gaining increasing recognition. A diverse workforce brings different perspectives and ideas, fostering innovation. Companies like IBM and Salesforce prioritize diversity in their hiring practices and corporate culture.

## 10. Ethical Considerations

Tech companies are increasingly addressing ethical considerations in their development processes. Ethical AI, responsible data usage, and sustainable practices are areas receiving attention. Developers should be aware of the ethical implications of their work and strive for responsible coding.

In conclusion, the programming world can draw valuable lessons from industry giants, including the importance of continuous learning, user-centric design, iterative development, automation, data-driven decision making, scalability, security, collaboration, diversity, and ethical considerations. By incorporating these lessons into their practices, developers can create better software, contribute to the tech community, and navigate the ever-changing landscape of programming effectively.

# Chapter 20: The Programmer's Journey: Learning and Mastering Languages

## Section 20.1: Strategies for Learning New Programming Languages

Learning new programming languages is an essential skill for every developer. Whether you're a beginner just starting your coding journey or an experienced programmer expanding your horizons, the ability to pick up new languages efficiently is valuable. In this section, we'll explore strategies and techniques to help you learn and master programming languages effectively.

### 1. Start with Fundamentals

Before diving into a new language, make sure you understand the fundamental concepts of programming. Familiarize yourself with data types, control structures, and basic algorithms. This foundation will make it easier to grasp language-specific features.

### 2. Choose the Right Language

Select a programming language that aligns with your goals and interests. If you're interested in web development, languages like JavaScript, Python, or Ruby may be suitable. For system programming, consider C or Rust. Learning a language relevant to your objectives will keep you motivated.

### 3. Utilize Online Resources

The internet is a treasure trove of resources for learning programming languages. Explore online courses, tutorials, and documentation. Platforms like Codecademy, Coursera, edX, and YouTube offer a wide range of programming courses.

### 4. Hands-On Practice

Theory alone won't make you proficient. Practice is crucial. Write code, build projects, and solve problems using the new language. Leverage coding challenges on platforms like LeetCode and HackerRank to reinforce your skills.

### 5. Work on Real Projects

Apply your knowledge by working on real-world projects. Start with small applications and gradually tackle more complex ones. Building practical projects enhances your problem-solving abilities and showcases your skills to potential employers.

### 6. Learn Language Features

Each programming language has its unique features and syntax. Focus on understanding these language-specific aspects. Pay attention to data structures, libraries, and frameworks commonly used in the language.

### 7. Read Code and Documentation

Study code written by experienced developers in the language you're learning. Reading open-source projects and documentation can provide insights into best practices and idiomatic expressions.

### 8. Join Coding Communities

Participate in coding communities and forums related to the language. Engage in discussions, ask questions, and seek help when needed. Learning from others and sharing your experiences can accelerate your progress.

### 9. Experiment and Tinker

Don't be afraid to experiment and make mistakes. Learning often involves trial and error. Tinkering with code and exploring different approaches can deepen your understanding.

### 10. Teach Others

Teaching is an effective way to solidify your knowledge. Share what you've learned with others, whether through mentoring, blogging, or creating tutorials. Teaching forces you to articulate concepts clearly.

### 11. Stay Persistent and Patient

Learning a new programming language takes time and effort. Stay persistent, be patient with yourself, and embrace the learning process. It's normal to encounter challenges along the way.

### 12. Stay Updated

Programming languages evolve, and new versions are released. Stay updated with language changes and best practices. Follow blogs, attend conferences, and subscribe to newsletters relevant to the language.

In conclusion, learning and mastering programming languages is a continuous journey. By starting with fundamentals, choosing the right language, utilizing online resources, practicing, working on projects, understanding language features, reading code, joining communities, experimenting, teaching others, being persistent, and staying updated, you can effectively add new languages to your skill set. Embrace the excitement of exploring new languages and the opportunities they bring to your programming career.

---

### Section 20.2: Balancing Breadth and Depth in Language Proficiency

As a programmer on your journey to learning and mastering programming languages, you'll encounter a common dilemma: whether to focus on acquiring broad knowledge across multiple languages or to dive deep into the intricacies of a single language. This section explores the concept of balancing breadth and depth in language proficiency.

Breadth: Exploring Multiple Languages

Learning multiple programming languages can be advantageous for several reasons:

1. **Versatility**: Different languages are designed for specific purposes. Acquiring proficiency in a variety of languages allows you to choose the most suitable tool for a particular task or project.

2. **Problem-Solving Skills**: Exposure to diverse languages exposes you to various programming paradigms and problem-solving approaches. This broadens your horizons and enhances your ability to tackle different types of challenges.

3. **Marketability**: A diverse skill set makes you more marketable to employers. Companies often seek developers who can adapt to different tech stacks and languages as project requirements evolve.

4. **Language Features**: Each language has unique features and strengths. Learning multiple languages helps you leverage these features effectively.

However, exploring multiple languages requires time and effort. Here are some strategies to balance breadth:

- **Focus on Fundamentals**: Ensure you have a strong foundation in programming fundamentals shared across languages, such as data structures and algorithms.

- **Choose Complementary Languages**: Select languages that complement each other. For example, learning both Python and SQL is valuable for data analysis.

- **Learn the Ecosystem**: Understand the libraries, frameworks, and tools commonly used with each language. Proficiency in the broader ecosystem can be as important as the language itself.

- **Stay Organized**: Keep a portfolio or documentation of your knowledge in each language. This helps you quickly reference syntax and features.

Depth: Mastering a Single Language

Alternatively, you can choose to dive deep into a single programming language. Becoming a master of a particular language has its advantages:

1. **Expertise**: In-depth knowledge of a language allows you to write efficient and optimized code. You can leverage advanced language features and design patterns effectively.

2. **Specialization**: Specializing in a specific language can open up niche career opportunities. For example, becoming a JavaScript expert could lead to roles in web development or Node.js-based backend development.

3. **Problem Domain**: Some languages are particularly well-suited for specific problem domains. Deep expertise in such a language positions you as an authority in that field.

4. **Community Contribution**: Deep knowledge enables you to contribute to the language's community, whether by creating libraries, writing documentation, or participating in open-source projects.

To achieve depth, consider the following:

- **In-Depth Study**: Dedicate focused time to study the language thoroughly. Explore advanced topics, best practices, and design patterns.

- **Build Projects**: Apply your knowledge by building complex projects in the chosen language. Real-world experience deepens your understanding.

- **Mentorship**: Seek mentorship or guidance from experts in the language. Learning from experienced practitioners can accelerate your mastery.

- **Stay Current**: Keep up with language updates, new libraries, and emerging patterns. Stagnation in a rapidly evolving language can be detrimental.

Ultimately, the decision to prioritize breadth or depth depends on your career goals and interests. Some developers choose to start with breadth and gradually specialize in a language, while others prefer to focus deeply on a language that aligns with their passion. Whichever path you choose, remember that the programming world is vast and continuously evolving, offering opportunities for both generalists and specialists.

---

## Section 20.3: Building a Personal Coding Portfolio

A personal coding portfolio is a powerful asset for any programmer, whether you're a beginner or an experienced developer. It serves as a showcase of your skills, projects, and accomplishments, making it a valuable tool for career development and self-improvement.

### Why Build a Coding Portfolio?

1. **Demonstrates Your Skills**: A portfolio allows you to demonstrate your coding skills, problem-solving abilities, and creativity to potential employers or clients. It's tangible proof of what you can do.

2. **Showcases Your Projects**: Whether it's a web application, a mobile app, or open-source contributions, your portfolio showcases real-world projects you've worked on. This helps others understand your practical experience.

3. **Highlights Your Specialization**: If you have a specific niche or specialization, your portfolio can emphasize this expertise. It positions you as an authority in your chosen domain.

4. **Personal Branding**: A well-curated portfolio contributes to your personal branding as a developer. It reflects your professionalism, attention to detail, and commitment to your craft.

5. **Learning and Growth**: Building a portfolio can be a continuous learning journey. Each project presents opportunities to acquire new skills and improve existing ones.

How to Build an Effective Portfolio

*1. Choose a Platform:*

Decide where you want to host your portfolio. Options include personal websites, GitHub Pages, or platforms like LinkedIn and Behance. Ensure the platform aligns with your goals and audience.

*2. Select Projects Wisely:*

Feature a mix of your best projects. Include personal projects, contributions to open-source, and work-related projects if possible. Highlight diverse skills and technologies.

*3. Provide Detailed Descriptions:*

For each project, provide descriptions that explain the problem you solved, the technologies used, your role, and the impact of the project. Use clear and concise language.

*4. Include Code Samples:*

If appropriate, share code snippets or link to GitHub repositories. This allows visitors to delve deeper into your code and assess your coding style.

*5. Showcase Results:*

Highlight the outcomes or results of your projects. Did it improve efficiency, solve a problem, or achieve a specific goal? Quantify the impact when possible.

*6. Maintain Consistency:*

Maintain a consistent visual theme and layout throughout your portfolio. Use high-quality images and ensure everything is well-organized.

*7. Highlight Learning and Growth:*

Include a section that showcases your journey as a developer. Discuss challenges you've overcome, new skills you've acquired, and your passion for coding.

*8. Contact Information:*

Make it easy for visitors to reach out to you. Provide clear contact information or links to your social profiles and email.

Regularly update your portfolio with new projects and experiences. An up-to-date portfolio demonstrates your commitment to ongoing learning and improvement.

*10. Gather Feedback:*

Seek feedback from peers, mentors, or online communities. Constructive feedback can help you refine your portfolio and make it more appealing.

Remember that building a coding portfolio is an ongoing process. As you gain more experience and complete new projects, continue to showcase your growth and expertise. Your portfolio is a dynamic representation of your skills and journey as a programmer, and it can play a significant role in advancing your career.

---

## Section 20.4: Staying Current with Technological Advances

In the fast-paced world of programming, staying current with technological advances is essential for both personal and professional growth. Technologies, languages, and tools evolve rapidly, and programmers must adapt to these changes to remain relevant and competitive in the field. Here are some strategies for staying up-to-date with the latest advancements:

### 1. Continuous Learning

Programming is a field where learning never stops. Commit to lifelong learning and dedicate time regularly to explore new technologies, programming languages, and frameworks. Online courses, tutorials, and documentation are excellent resources for acquiring new knowledge.

### 2. Follow Industry Trends

Subscribe to tech news websites, blogs, and newsletters that cover industry trends and developments. Platforms like Hacker News, Reddit, and Stack Overflow can provide valuable insights into what's trending in the tech world.

### 3. Attend Conferences and Meetups

Tech conferences, meetups, and webinars are great opportunities to network with peers and learn about the latest innovations. Many conferences offer online versions, making it easier to attend regardless of your location.

### 4. Join Online Communities

Participate in online programming communities, such as GitHub, GitLab, and programming-related subreddits. Engaging with other developers can lead to discussions about new technologies and best practices.

### 5. Experiment with Side Projects

Working on side projects allows you to experiment with new technologies in a practical context. It's a hands-on way to learn and stay updated while building something meaningful.

### 6. Read Books and Documentation

Books and official documentation are valuable sources of in-depth knowledge. Consider reading books authored by experts in your field or exploring the documentation of languages and frameworks you use.

### 7. Online Courses and Tutorials

Online learning platforms like Coursera, edX, and Udemy offer a wide range of courses on various programming topics. Enroll in courses that cover emerging technologies to gain expertise.

### 8. Contribute to Open Source

Contributing to open-source projects allows you to collaborate with experienced developers and work on projects that use the latest technologies. It's a practical way to learn and make a meaningful impact.

### 9. Follow Thought Leaders

Identify thought leaders and influential figures in the programming community. Follow them on social media, read their blogs, and listen to their podcasts for insights and recommendations.

### 10. Build a Personal Learning Plan

Create a personalized learning plan that outlines your goals and the technologies you want to master. Break it down into manageable steps and track your progress.

### 11. Embrace New Challenges

Don't shy away from new challenges and opportunities at work or in personal projects. Taking on tasks that require you to learn and adapt can be a rewarding way to stay current.

### 12. Network with Peers

Networking with fellow programmers can lead to valuable discussions about emerging technologies and best practices. Attend local meetups or virtual networking events.

### 13. Stay Inquisitive

Maintain a curious mindset and ask questions when you encounter something unfamiliar. Being inquisitive is a fundamental trait of successful programmers.

Remember that staying current with technological advances is an ongoing commitment. Embrace change as an opportunity for growth and innovation. By adopting these strategies and remaining adaptable, you can ensure that you continue to thrive in the dynamic world of programming.

---

## Section 20.5: Fostering a Lifelong Passion for Coding

Coding is not just a profession; it's a passion for many programmers. Fostering a lifelong passion for coding can significantly enhance your career and personal satisfaction. Here are some tips to help you maintain and nurture your enthusiasm for programming:

### 1. Build Meaningful Projects

One of the best ways to stay passionate about coding is to work on projects that matter to you. Whether it's a personal website, a mobile app, or a game, building something meaningful can keep your interest alive.

### 2. Collaborate with Others

Programming doesn't have to be a solitary activity. Collaborating with others on coding projects can bring fresh perspectives and new ideas, making the process more enjoyable.

### 3. Stay Curious

Never stop being curious. Keep asking questions, exploring new technologies, and seeking answers. The thrill of discovery can reignite your passion.

### 4. Teach and Mentor

Sharing your knowledge with others can be incredibly rewarding. Teaching or mentoring someone, whether it's a colleague or a student, can remind you of the excitement of learning and help you appreciate your expertise.

### 5. Participate in Coding Challenges

Coding challenges and competitions, such as Hackathons and coding contests, can be both fun and intellectually stimulating. They provide opportunities to test your skills and learn from others.

### 6. Explore Different Domains

Programming can be applied in various domains, from game development to data science and robotics. Exploring different areas can open up new horizons and interests.

### 7. Read and Write Code Regularly

Just like any skill, coding improves with practice. Regularly reading and writing code can keep your skills sharp and your passion alive.

```python
def main():
    print("Hello, World!")

if __name__ == "__main__":
    main()
```

### 8. Attend Tech Events

Tech conferences, workshops, and meetups can expose you to the latest trends and innovations in the industry. Being part of a community can be motivating.

### 9. Set Personal Goals

Challenge yourself with personal coding goals. It could be mastering a new language, contributing to an open-source project, or building a specific application.

### 10. Celebrate Your Achievements

Take time to acknowledge and celebrate your coding achievements, no matter how small. Recognizing your progress can boost your motivation.

### 11. Stay Informed

Stay updated on industry news, programming languages, and emerging technologies. Being informed can help you see the bigger picture and the possibilities.

### 12. Balance Work and Life

Maintaining a healthy work-life balance is crucial for preventing burnout and preserving your passion for coding. Don't forget to relax and recharge.

### 13. Join Coding Communities

Engage with coding communities online or offline. Sharing experiences, challenges, and successes with like-minded individuals can be inspiring.

### 14. Explore Creative Coding

Experiment with creative coding and art projects. Mixing art and technology can be a refreshing change from traditional coding tasks.

Consider keeping a coding journal where you document your coding journey, ideas, and reflections. It can serve as a source of inspiration and a record of your progress.

Fostering a lifelong passion for coding is not only about career success but also about personal fulfillment. Remember that it's normal to have ups and downs in your coding journey, but by staying curious and embracing the joy of creation, you can enjoy a rewarding and enduring relationship with programming.

www.ingramcontent.com/pod-product-compliance
Lightning Source LLC
LaVergne TN
LVHW051325050326
832903LV00031B/3361